Good Puppy Academics

Good Puppy Academics

Academics

USING NATURE'S WAY TO RAISE YOUR DOG'S **GPA**

Margie Cantwell

To order additional copies of this book, contact:
Xlibris Corporation
1-888-795-4274
www.Xlibris.com
Orders@Xlibris.com
114625

CONTENTS

INTRODUCTION

THIS BOOK WAS written for people who feel overwhelmed, confused, or simply "turned off" by all the conflicting dog training methods available to us today. There is so much information (created by people) on the subject that it is difficult to sort out who's right, who's wrong, what works, and what doesn't work. I have designed this simple book to touch on the basic things that *apply to all dogs and their owners* because it's not my way, it's nature's way—a sensible, universal place to start regardless of what kind of dog or puppy you have because it's encoded in their genes.

In the chapters to follow, I *briefly* touch on *critical subjects,* presented in short sections, for you to further research and *gain an even better understanding* of the awesome power of nature's way. These critical subjects are like whole other volumes to this book because the more you understand the science of learning and the mind the easier it is to incorporate these in your everyday life. So take the time to school yourself on the subjects and methods mentioned throughout this book as I do not elaborate on them; I just bring them to light for you.

There are many experienced and reliable dog trainers who understand and practice the topics found in this book and countless resources in print and on the Internet to learn from. You can even take a class on the subjects that interest you. The more you learn about your dog the more you will learn about yourself because it is they who taught us what we now know about ourselves.

WHO AM I?

WHEN I WAS around ten years old, I received a Reader's Digest book from my mother titled *Our Amazing World of Nature*. In that book, I learned about the most fascinating things that animals could do—from polar bears able to cross a sheet of ice too thin to support a man to animals that use different strategies to survive and thrive in different environments. "Wow!" I thought. *Mother Nature made animals clever,* so they would be able to figure all this survival stuff out. I was intrigued *and I still am* because animals are cleverer than us in so many ways.

I had rats as pets and loved interacting with them. I would train them to do things for food and found communicating with my rodent friends very entertaining. We always had cats, but my parents were not ready for the responsibilities of a dog, so I'd borrow Country, the black Lab across the street to play with. Then one Mother's Day, my sister Brigitte and I gave my mother a German Shepherd mix puppy. I was eleven years old, and finally, we had our own dog! My mother named her Cora.

Cora and I spent the next six years together, running around the neighborhood like kids do. I was fascinated by the canine movie star Benji at the time, so Cora became my first entertainment dog. I could shoot her dead, make her stop wagging her tail on cue, and put a biscuit on her nose and make her wait before she would flip it into her mouth when told to. We were known around the neighborhood. I thought I had the smartest dog in the world (So did the neighborhood kids!).

Like many children of my age, I wanted to train animals when I grew up because "I thought I had a way with them."

Looking back, I realize that I was simply tapping into a science known as operant conditioning and classical conditioning to train my rats and dog. I was just doing what came naturally because it felt right and worked. It was spontaneous and simple to train that way. It was as if the animal was guiding the training through its feedback. I would try different ways to get results to teach a new skill, based on the animal's responses. Their feedback became their voice. It was like having a conversation inspired and directed by the animal. Children are naturals at tapping into this since their lives are not yet cluttered with the stresses that adults deal with in their heads all day. The *primitive mind* is very active and alive in young children.

After I left home, I moved to Monterey, California, and started working in a small privately owned pet shop called Pet Paradise. That was 1981. Exotic bird training became my specialty (one that I still consider my favorite). I eventually moved on, and in spring of 1994, I received a bachelor's degree in liberal studies to teach elementary schoolchildren and a concentration in psychology and communication. Little did I know then that the foundation was being set for where my journey has taken me today.

Like many people with a degree, I put those talents aside and settled for a career in the hotel industry, where I spent the next eight years loving my job but feeling as if I needed something more meaningful and fulfilling to wake up to. Then I moved to Northern California, where I discovered an amazing organization that trained dogs to help people in wheelchairs. That organization was Canine Companions for Independence (CCI) in Santa Rosa, California.

I signed up to volunteer right away. That was in 1998. I volunteered at their Santa Rosa national headquarters for five years and became so moved by how a dog can liberate someone's life that I knew I had to become part of it. *This was worth getting up for every morning.* I decided to apply for CCI's new trainer intern program that had just started hiring. I knew it was a long shot, but I tried anyway. I did get the interview, but unfortunately, I did not get the job. Little did I know then that not getting hired would turn out to be a blessing in disguise. As one door closed, another, even better, door opened.

Determined to change career paths, I turned to the only place in the world (literally) which offers a degree on how to train assistance dogs—the Assistance Dog Institute, now known as Bergin University of Canine Studies, located on a beautiful new campus in Rohnert Park, California. I applied to their assistance dog education associate degree program, was accepted, and started in fall of 2003. The schooling I received at the Assistance Dog Institute *was priceless.* Not only did I learn everything I needed to know on how to properly train a service dog and start a nonprofit organization like CCI, but I learned it all from Dr. Bonnie Bergin, creator of the service dog concept and founder of CCI!

This was my opportunity. When I started my classes at the Assistance Dog Institute, I found so much in common with the BA degree I already had. Little did I know then that child development, psychology, and communication skills were what helped to make the service dog concept work in 1975 when Bonnie Bergin, an educator not a dog trainer, spawned the idea that she could train a dog to help someone with severe mobility impairments, knowing how independence could improve their life by giving them a greater sense of well-being and acceptance while being actively independent out in society.

The 1970s was a hotbed of studies and seminars in psychology and learning. To be an effective educator, Bonnie

Bergin had to keep up-to-date on these studies. Knowledge on how schoolchildren learn best had been scientifically proven, and physical punishment, such as paddling a student or degrading them in front of their peers, which had been a common practice in schools for centuries, was now being challenged and frowned upon. Thus, other methods of teaching and discipline had to be put into place in our public school systems.

Teachers that practiced the old-school tactics of negative reinforcement either changed their ways or, like today, faced being challenged by students and their parents, as the use of *learning theory* was becoming the new norm for teaching, since it encompasses the study of the many principles and mechanisms of learning. These various learning theories came from the field of psychology and were discovered and expressed by people like Wilhelm Wundt in 1879. Known as the "father of psychology," he gave us insight into what is known as *cognitive learning theory,* a detailed look at how the brain processes information and uses it. Then there was John Watson in 1913 who introduced us to the behaviorist view, where just observable behaviors were the key to understanding what makes us do the things we do.

There were scientists like B. F. Skinner, who introduced us to operant conditioning, and Ivan Pavlov, the father of classical conditioning, and many others working on finding different angles to how we learn and what learning is. All of them had a huge impact on our understanding of the psychological processes in animals with a brain. These are the different *learning theories* and are important to understand to be an efficient and effective instructor *no matter whom or what you teach.*

Teachers in the 1970s were being educated on these methods through studies, seminars, and books in order to give them the proper tools to use on their students. They had to understand

and implement many different learning theories into the mix since children are not robots and learn differently. Theories like *simple non-associative learning, habituation, enculturation, rote learning, imprinting, sensitization, associative learning, classical conditioning, operant conditioning, observational learning, play, episodic learning, meaningful learning, informal learning, transfer of learning, metacognition* were all being integrated in the 1970s and 1980s into our schools around the country as more parents demanded their children learn in a non-abusive, motivational environment.

With this science backing her, Bonnie Bergin recognized that the dog's capabilities and natural attraction to reward were similar to a young child's and saw the potential in using the same positive enforcement and motivational methods she utilized with her human students to influence her canine ones. It is this approach that helped to make the service dog concept possible in its earliest beginnings. People who worked with the disabled at the time believed that what Bonnie Bergin was attempting was impossible for a disabled person. After all, conventional dog training methods require much physical handling of the dog something a person with severe mobility impairment in a wheelchair cannot and should not have to do. It was viewed as just too dangerous.

Bonnie Bergin realized this early on since the original service dogs she created were first trained and intended for use by people in wheelchairs that had extremely limited mobility in their arms and/or legs. That's why Bonnie knew that intimidating dog training methods could never work. She had to find a different approach and thought she could use her knowledge and passion as an educator to train dogs by verbal command that would respond to their handler willingly, eagerly, and reliably without any physical intervention from their human partner once trained. Bonnie Bergin incorporated the dog's mind and emotions (in the 1970s, science had us believing that animals had no feelings or emotions) into the learning process.

Rather than focusing solely on physical correction, rote memory, and negative reinforcement techniques commonly used to train dogs (and children) *for centuries*, Bonnie spent years working with different types of dogs and trainers to better understand the balance she needed to have in order to reach her final goal of producing a reliable helpmate that could change somebody's life. Dog trainers using intimidation or negative reinforcement to "master their beasts" and the trainers who understood the dog's mind and were already combining traditional dog training concepts coupled with positive reinforcement, all gave Bonnie a better understanding as to how she could fine-tune the service dog to what it has become today. *She was able to weed out what was constructive to the human-canine bond and what was destructive* based on her experiences over many years of observing different styles of training methods. Without finding the right balance, the service dog concept never could have developed as it did and continues to today.

Bonnie Bergin understood then that the science of setting the neural pathways in the brain by using positive reinforcement instead of rote training and negative reinforcement was the key to producing a truly reliable canine companion. A service dog that was "hardwired" to do their job *because they problem-solved to set the neural pathways in their brain like nature would have it,* not just wired to memorize it through *human will.*

As a result of her work, Bonnie Bergin created and placed the world's first service dog, named Abdul, with a severely disabled quadriplegic woman affected by muscular dystrophy. Her name is Kerry Knaus, and with her help, the first service dog team was created in 1975. Since then, improvements in the way service dogs are chosen, trained, and handled have evolved dramatically thanks to Bonnie's years of trials and determination to realize her vision of training service dogs without using traditional negative reinforcement methods. It really is a remarkable success story.

Kerry and Abdul. The first Canine Companion for Independence service dog team paved the way for all service dog users today.

I was graduated from the Assistance Dog Institute in spring 2004 and moved to the Central Valley of California. On August 1, 2004, I founded Service Dogs for Self-Reliance a 501(c) (3) nonprofit organization and became a provisional member of Assistance Dogs International. I am the founder of the *Rx Pharmdog* concept, as well as *psychiatricservicedogs. com*, the most comprehensive service dog training website in the world. I am an evaluator for the American Kennel Club Canine Good Citizen's program, and I specialize in training service dog public access behaviors and task training as well as early puppy skill development. I train pets and their guardians as well.

I feel fortunate to have been "hardwired" by Bonnie Bergin's influence on service dog training since it has truly served me and my subjects well to be able to actually use my bachelor degree in teaching in conjunction with the schooling of my canine and human subjects. What the animals have taught us about ourselves in laboratories is finally coming back to them full circle. Many animals have suffered for the sake of science to teach us what we now know about ourselves. It's time for *all of us* to give it back so they too can reap the benefits of what they have been teaching us about ourselves for years.

BUT THAT'S NOT REALLY WHO I AM

T O A DOG, my education and experiences mean nothing. Animals are not impressed by our accomplishments. A dog doesn't care if you live in a homeless camp or Hollywood mansion or if you have a PhD or GED. It makes no difference to a dog. *So who am I really?* Certainly not who you think I am.

Humans live in a world dogs don't understand. Dogs don't evaluate you by your history. They evaluate you by the energy (or vibe) you are putting out and by your body language. It's how the "primitive" mind works. I use the term *primitive mind* to describe the part of the brain that is not caught up in anything but the moment. It knows nothing else. Driven by the *instinctual and intuitional hardware* of the inner brain, it's the mind that is not preoccupied with paying bills or having to be at work on time and does not rationalize about yesterday or tomorrow. It just exists in the moment. It's the mind that we "high-tech" intelligent human beings are using less and less of in this high stress, money-driven life we lead, where there is no place for the primitive mind to thrive except maybe in a yoga class if you are able to tap into it over all the static in your life and mind. We have become so out of tune with our primitive mind; it changes who we really are inside ourselves.

Dogs are so in tuned to their environments that I like to say, "Dogs can sense your thoughts." I say this because with every thought you have, your brain emits chemical and electrical signals (synapses) that make you unconsciously convey your thoughts through your body language and the airborne compounds (chemical scent) your body releases. This innate ability tells a dog who you *really are* in that moment. For example, if you are trying to be patient but are thinking in your head "this stupid dog will never learn how to sit," your dog will most likely never learn to sit. For one thing you will never succeed in convincing him that he can do it if even you don't think he can, and your dog will be wondering why you are so stressed over the word *sit*, driving his focus and interest further away from the lesson. In other words, you can't lie to a dog. They know who you really are, and you can't fool them.

Just by changing your thoughts, the rest follows. But you must practice it to make it work. It is an old spiritual principle that works on anything you can imagine. Countless people and cultures around the world have been practicing and living by these principles since the beginning of human civilization. *It's Mother Nature's way* to help us get things done. Visualizing the end result allows you to see the success before it happens which drives you to achieve the end result you desire. It's like a self-fulfilling prophecy. Your dog will sense your confidence in him and be more willing to connect with you if only you believe in him and your ability to teach him.

The power of your thoughts can work for or against you when training any animal, including yourself. *I believe dogs are often in our lives as a test*—here to help us see our strengths and face our weaknesses. If we just let them, dogs can teach us some good lessons about what's inside ourselves. What lessons can your dog teach you? I can't tell you. But I know they will be lessons to learn from. Better than any I could ever teach you. Because *there are some things only a dog can teach when human intervention fails*. So let go and let dog. You might be surprised at the feedback you get.

In developed countries like ours, we have gotten so sophisticated with our artificial creations that, in my opinion, those of us who live in these incredible developed nations have become somewhat freaks of nature. There are millions, if not billions, of people living on this planet who still live as our ancestors have for thousands of years, in sync with nature. Most of these people live in underdeveloped countries and many in developed countries, occupying villages in isolated rain forests or on the open plains where life is lived day by day, in the best interests of the moment. Unfortunately, some of these people are caught up in other people's daily interests fueled by money and politics, so life for them is a different kind of survival. In this world, there are many ways to lose touch with the source of ourselves. *We must appreciate that it's there for us regardless of our circumstances.* But we must tap into it first.

We human beings, who live in these rich and powerful countries with supermarkets for hunting grounds and electricity providing light when our brain needs dark, are living like no other century before us. Our survival has become a money game. We are dependent on utilities, a steady job, cars, media, instant gratification, paying rent, paying, paying, and paying some more until you have paid enough to keep a roof over your head in your old age, since family values can't always be counted on these days. Many elderly people today have no family members willing or able to care for them as a result of our busy "currency" centered lives. This is hardly how nature intended us to thrive in this world as the family-oriented species that we are meant to be.

But don't get me wrong. I feel privileged to live in such a convenient powerful society. I don't know how to live differently. I depend on all this technology and love it. But it does change who we really are as "primitive" human beings. *There is no place for our primitive selves to flourish here* because it's smothered by the demands of keeping up with all the pressures of living in our society, getting us further out of touch with our most basic nature and affecting our very being. We must tap back into the primitive part of ourselves if we are to understand how an animal thinks and sees the world around it, because *we have become complicated while they have remained simple.*

Animals have been here so much longer than us. Like their ancestors before them, animals continue to be strongly influenced by the primitive nature of their genes. We too are animals. But our primitive nature has been overwhelmed with too much "human" garbage. *I don't want that to be who I am.* My dog keeps me balanced when I see my strengths and weaknesses through him. The feedback I get from my dog when we communicate says a lot about me. It's the beauty that's in your dog that's important, not what he looks like on the outside. My dog reminds me every day to tap into the wild within me and live in the moment and be resilient and determined; then the rest will follow because that's nature's way.

CHAPTER 1

Gray wolf (*Canis Lupus*). *Al Gagnon/Dreamstime.com*

What's in a Dog?
(Who Are They?)

FROM BIRTH TO age three, human infants are developing to reach milestones that are age appropriate. So is your dog. However, your dog goes through their infant, toddler, and teens in the first two years of their life. So by age two, dogs are considered adults, and at seven years old, they are considered early seniors. So dogs develop much faster than our human children do since their life span is shorter.

As adults, most dogs' cognitive abilities will only reach the equivalent of a three-year-old human child's level. So their cognitive mind never develops past that point as it reaches the milestones you would expect for their species. Some three-year-old children are brighter than others, just like some dogs are. That's Mother Nature's design. The only part we play is in bringing out their individual potential. In nature, it's never about being "smarter." It's about being stable and successful at whatever level you are at. In nature, the prize goes to the ones who problem-solve and endure adversity. These are the winners. Smart is an individual thing. Smart isn't needed to endure adversity. Flexibility and perseverance are essential.

It's important to understand who your dog really is on the inside if you are going to be successful in training and handling it. Why is this true? The reality is that your dog is a predator since 99.8 percent of its mitochondrial DNA is identical to the Asian gray wolf. Predators rely on their keen sense of being able to read an animal's body language in order to succeed at outmaneuvering it during the hunt and ultimately the kill.

This ability is encoded in your dog's DNA. It's the 99.8 percent "wild within" that came with the package deal when we succeeded in altering 0.2 percent of the wolf's genes into something we could domesticate. Knowing how to influence and motivate your subjects through communication that brings out their true potential is the key to being a great animal trainer. You must gain a good perspective into your dog's mind and understand his language and view of the world to effectively interact with him in a way *a dog can understand.*

Kayleigh, Bella, and Luka play much like wolf pups and adolescents would, with no harm done, testing boundaries and status among themselves. *Photo by: Julie Aitken.*

While we share the same physical space with our dogs, *only 0.2 percent of the dog shares its mental space with you.* The other 99.8 percent is shared with nature. That 0.2 percent alteration, however, has been encoded with things that make the domestic dog very different than its ancestor, the wolf. Over the last fifteen thousand years, domestic dogs have been studying humans as if we were packmates, having to learn our body language, pheromone signals, and other cues we emit unconsciously. Something a wild wolf has no interest in.

Humans are not considered family to a wild wolf pack because humans are not encoded in their genes that way. Even wolves that were raised from birth like domestic dogs act differently than their domesticated cousins when it comes to interpreting human signals. Their genes interpret us in a more primitive way. As outsiders, the way *nature* intended by design.

When wild or captive wolves do accept human company, it's *always* on their terms not ours. You cannot force human will on a wolf. They will not respond like a domestic dog will. In the wild, it is *extremely* rare for humans to be preyed on by wolfs. It just doesn't happen in a balanced echo system. It is only the captive animals who are a danger to humans, and the ones we challenge by putting our self-interests before theirs when we keep them as pets or build our homes and ranches in their territories. So we blame the wolf for being dangerous or in the way of *our* precious profits to justify eliminating them from the wild. Did you know that by 1990, there were only about fifty wild wolves left in the western United States? So next time you look at your pet dog, think about how unfair we are being to their kin. Without the wolf, none of us would have a dog to love us unconditionally.

Because your dog's DNA is 99.8 percent identical to the mitochondrial DNA of the Asian gray wolf, the slight 0.2 percent of genetic modifications we have created over the last fifteen thousand years has resulted in domestication. So every dog, regardless of the breed, size, or gender, is genetically programmed to do some or all of the following behaviors: *jump, bite, dig, nip, destructive chewing, whine, poop, pee, run, explore, eat disgusting things, roll in gross smells, tracking, chasing, fight, flight, avoidance, submission, resource guarding, howling, licking, and so on.* It's the 99.8 percent wild within. And most people don't like it.

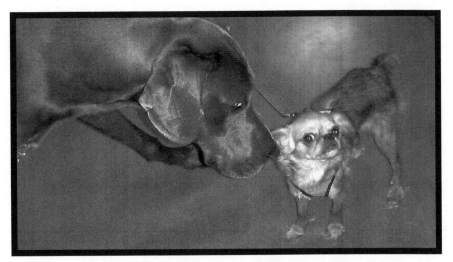

Great Dane puppy Sophia has a head that is bigger than her little friend Crystal's whole body!

The domestic dog (*Canis lupus familiaris*) is a species of the Canidae family. Domestic canines are the only animals on earth whose size, shape, and breed specific traits are so varied. No other animal in nature has such variations. That's because the canine's genes lend themselves to a wide variety of manipulations, which is known in genetic science as "*genetic plasticity to mutations in tandem repeats.*"

Tandem repeats are small sections of DNA that repeat themselves causing changes to the organism. Only in the canine species, this flexibility in the genes is so malleable or "slippery" as it's called in genetics. These tandem repeats are what give us the Great Dane all the way down to the teacup Poodle. English Bulldogs and the Brussels Griffon are a great example of a "look" that could be mistaken as an entirely different species of dog compared to the Husky or German Shepherd dog that no doubt resembles their wild cousin the wolf. In fact, over the last two centuries, the explosion of new breeds has been so diverse; we have altered the whole physical look of the dog through *eugenics.*

Gray wolf. *Dmitrij/Dreamstime.com*

Siberian Husky Sammie.

Bulldog Lola.

Brussels Griffon Ruthy.

German Shepherd Rex.

But that's not the whole story. It's possible that domestication was a rapid process rather than a long drawn out one according to a Russian fox study started in the late 1940s by a Soviet genetic scientist named Dmitri Belyaev. A fox farm in Moscow that raised silver foxes (*Vulpes vulpes*), also a member of the Canidae family, for the fur industry hired Belyaev to see if he could produce a more submissive fox since the wild ones they were breeding and raising for the fur trade were very dangerous and hard to handle. Dmitri Belyaev started this breeding program by choosing foxes to breed that were the least fearful of humans. After only ten generations of selective breeding for tameness, almost one-fifth of the new population of silver foxes had become domesticated enough to handle safely. But something unexpected happened in the process.

Silver Fox. *Mikael Males/Dreamstime.com*

Over time, this new strain of domesticated silver foxes began taking on the characteristic of our domestic dogs. Their ears went from being erect to bending over and becoming floppy; their straight tails began to curl, and the color of their fur changed and even became spotted. They, in fact, began taking on and retaining puppy-like traits. Dmitri Belyaev was interested in *Mendelian genetics*. The study of how certain traits are passed on to offspring from their parents.

Dmitri Belyaev believed that behavior was influenced by one's biology, so by selecting the tamest animals, he was, in fact, selecting against the body's hormones and neurochemicals that feed aggression in favor of the chemicals that make you more willing and able to create physiological changes that make an animal more docile and willing to submit to human interactions. This idea cost him his job due to politics, but by 1959, Dmitri Belyaev found himself in Siberia as the director of the Institute of Cytology and Genetics, where he continued the silver fox breeding program and studying the process of domestication in the silver foxes. Although Dmitri Belyaev died in 1985, his study continues today.

Because some behavior is rooted in biology, selecting for tameness and against aggression means selecting for physiological changes in the animal. Tinkering with nature by selecting the most passive animals gave this submissive gene a chance to thrive and reproduce under human intervention. Aggression is intended as a survival trait. A wild animal that is submissive either dies early or lives but is less likely to breed and pass its genes on.

With the exception of the elephant, there are no wild animals on earth with floppy ears. In nature, erect ears are needed to hear every sound possible. Having a strong fight or flight response is also critical. Today, these domesticated silver foxes have become so tame, after over fifty years of selective breeding, that they are commonly sold as pets to fund the continuing research. This is a breakthrough in understanding the power of the brain and the processes which control the body's hormones and neurochemicals. It is a fascinating science.

It had long been a mystery as to how domestic dogs got coats that are so different in coloration than their wild cousins the gray wolf. Tricolor, brindle, and spotted coats are not present in the wolf. In fact, this variety in color and pattern is something not seen in the same species anywhere in the natural world. It was eventually noted that this change was caused by having a low dose of the chemical *adrenaline* in the animal's *fight and flight responses*. It made sense. By selecting only the foxes that exhibited the least fear of humans, Dmitri Belyaev was inadvertently choosing the foxes whose adrenaline was not as high as their more aggressive relatives. Being afraid of humans and having a strong flight response are vital to the survival of both wild animals and us.

Not having to live as a wild animal and living in sync with human beings as family members and caretakers does not require adrenaline for survival. In fact, adrenaline works against you in this situation. There's an old saying, "Don't bite the hand that feeds you." For a dog whose life depends on human intervention for survival, this saying really rings true. Aggressive dogs are not accepted in society because of the danger they pose to the best interest of the population. That's why wolves are illegal to have as pets and also unwelcomed in our society.

Look at the domestic animals around you: sheep look like sheep; horses look like horses; chickens look like chickens; cats—while some variety in facial structure, color, and coat is present, domestic cats are all about the same size as adults, 10-20 lbs—are all equally suited to jump great heights, pounce, hunt, kill, be independent, and bury their scat (cats are not as domesticated as dogs). A leopard is a big cat. But unlike the Great Dane and Chihuahua, it's not the same species as your pet cat.

Leopard. *Lori Martin/Dreamstime.com*

Domestic cat. *Red2000/Dreamstime.com*

The Brain Game

The brain, whether human or canine, is an amazing phenomenon. The more you know how it works the easier it is to program it. When you are communicating with your dog, those cute whiskers, soulful eyes, and wagging tail are all you see. But that's just the outside of your dog, but *what's inside your dog is really who they are.* I believe you must train an animal from the inside out not the outside in if you are to communicate with them on *their* level. Let me explain what I mean.

There are currently around four hundred recognized dog breeds in the world, and countless combinations of "designer dogs" (hybrids) and so-called mutts (mixed breed) that make up the nearly half a billion dogs in the world today. All these domestic dogs were originally *genetically designed* by human intervention (eugenics) to perform a specific purpose in life. You must understand that purpose in order to train and stimulate them properly since their *genetic disposition* is hardwired into their brains. It's this awesome beauty that resides in each and every dog that is often overlooked or disliked by the pet owner. If you choose the wrong dog for your lifestyle, the chances are you won't enjoy your dog and your dog will not enjoy you either.

As you learn, neuroassociations are made, and new neural pathways are created in the brain. An animal's genetic disposition is hardwired and lies within the deepest structure of the brain. It is like the hardware in your computer system, storing the programs needed to run the rest of the machine efficiently. Behavioral influences become the software that can influence the hardware and the storage ability.

It's the relationship between the hardware and the software that makes the brain so adaptable and influential. An animal's genetic disposition can't be changed, but the environment that the animal lives in is a major influence. Because the nervous system must respond quickly and spontaneously to the environment around it, flexibility and change occur—it is this arrangement which makes the nervous system such a powerful mechanism, and it is important to know how and when to engage it properly. I call the process of participation *the brain game.*

Boxer puppy Cocoa.

This is exactly why being "cute," or feeling sorry, is no reason to choose a dog. Some dogs are not so cute after you bring them home and don't give them what *they need* to do well and thrive in *your* environment. Many end up in shelters and are euthanized. Even purebred dogs that end up homeless are euthanized on a daily basis. It's not just mutts anymore. You must look at what's within them first, to find the right match for you. That is your responsibility.

Dogs are what we made them. *Chemical and electrical synapses* (pathways), which are *neurological* (nature), and *outside influences* (nurture), which program us *psychologically* (life experiences), are things that influence the wiring of an animal's brain and must be understood if you are to teach any creature in a productive and humane way. So how do we take advantage of this knowledge to train the brain? Let's start by understanding the most overlooked part of the learning process, neurochemical, and electrical synapses.

The science of neurochemistry has been around since the 1950s and continues evolving today, and although complex, its premise is actually very simple. As I mentioned before, whenever you learn something, a *neuroassociation* is made, and a new *neural pathway* is created in the brain. The more you repeat the new behavior the more embedded the pathway becomes. The less you stimulate the pathway the less active it becomes. Think of a path through grass that is worn into the ground from all the traffic it sees. The more it gets used the more *prevalent* it becomes. But as soon as it stops being used, other elements in the environment *take over* until the path gets overgrown, and you can no longer notice it.

That doesn't mean it's still not there under the overgrowth. It just means that the overgrowth is just more prevalent now. It's the same with a neural pathway in the brain. Keep using the same neural pathway, and it will continue to be the path (behavior) most embedded and used. Change the undesired neural pathway (behavior), and the old neural pathway will eventually become less embedded and used as the new neural pathway embeds, and the overgrowth begins to change the animal's behavior. This is why behaviors can be altered by reconditioning or reprogramming these neural associations into something you like. This is powerful science, and dog trainers who don't understand it are behind in the times.

Neuroassociations are chemical and electrical synapses (circuits) found in the brain. *Chemical synapses* allow neurons to form circuits in the central nervous system, while *electrical synapses* link them with *a bridge of electrical current* (hardwired) to connect the neurons, so they can receive the *chemical signals being sent to form the circuit* (pathway). The brain is Mother Nature's computer, and it outdoes any of our modern machines. It's a phenomenal and sensible design, and we have the ability to influence it in many ways.

As nature would have it, all animals, including us, are genetically hardwired to gravitate toward things that bring us pleasure and reward and stay away from things that don't reward us or cause discomfort. This is the basic necessity for survival. *So the brain can be conditioned to respond to either pain or pleasure.* Using negative reinforcement capitalizes on the *pain factor* as the motivator. Using pinch collars, choke chains, and intimidation to assert your leadership and *force your will on the animal.* While positive reinforcement *capitalizes on reward* (pleasure) being the main motivator. *Positive punishment* and *negative punishment* are used in place of negative reinforcement to give the animal a fair choice of consequences to choose and learn from as nature would. This is what I am referring to when I use the term *nature's way.*

As you have learned, some of these neural pathways are biologically hardwired, and they express themselves in specific ways. Certain breeds need certain things (including mutts). If you know what that breed's genetic hardware is "hardwired" to do, then you know how that brain works, and you can use this knowledge to your benefit. If you try to make a dog be something it was never meant to be, like asking the English Bulldog to pull a sled through snow, then you will fail at bringing out the best in your dog, and your dog will fail to get pleasure out of doing what you're asking him to do. So what if your dog is a "mutt" or hybrid? Well, it's simple. Just observe what your dog enjoys doing, and he will tell you what he is "hardwired" to do. Also, your mutt's physical features can give you clues to his genetics and why he exhibits certain behaviors.

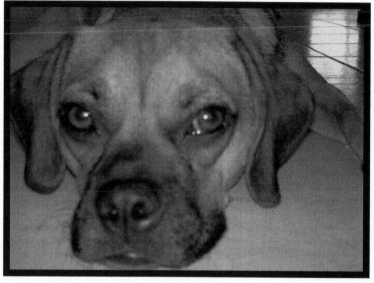

Designer dog Charlie, is a Puggle; a mix between a pug and a beagle. What innate behaviors can you expect? Pug or Beagle or both? Only time will tell.

If your dog has long, floppy ears and likes to sniff the ground a lot, it's probably got scent hound in its genes. If it's tall, lean, and runs fast, it could have some sight hound in its genes. Pricked ears and blue eyes could mean herding or sledding dog background. Brindle coats suggest some type of Bully breed is present somewhere in the distant or current gene pool, and so on. From the bloodhound whose genetic hardware has it following scent trails to the King Charles spaniel and the pampered Papillion whose ever-loving ability to sit on your lap all day, instead of following scent trails, makes it a better pet than hunting dog.

You need to know what type of dog is right for you. Rescuing a dog is wonderful but not because you feel sorry for it or you think it's cute. If it's not a good match for your lifestyle and you're not willing to change your lifestyle to accommodate the dog's needs, than be sure you rescue the *right dog* that meets *your needs* because a dog can't alter his genetic disposition to your liking once you bring him home.

Pit bull mix Bella enjoys getting energy out on her daily walks and other outdoor activities so she can enjoy her downtime when left home alone.

Every domestic dog at one time was a mutt bred to have a purpose. All purebred dogs are a result of mixing different dogs to get an end result that would allow mankind to use the genetically modified version *to advance himself.* In fact, in the past, people couldn't afford to feed dogs that didn't work for them. If a working dog didn't have the temperament it took to master the skills needed to do the job, it was not valued as a pet; instead, it was seen as having no place and eliminated from the next gene pool since there were no animal rescues or shelters back then. The wolf was first domesticated to use in the hunt and as protectors of their human pack. They were not domesticated to be pets that we simply indulge, admire, and enjoy.

Human beings always have been attracted to the animals around them. Early man may have tried to make a pet out of a baby wolf, but chances are he didn't always pick the right temperament pup every time since a wolf's genetic nature of being passive for humans is an oddity. He must have learned through trial and error trying to find the right balance between hunter and pet, choosing the pups with the right combination to breed. Like Dmitri Belyaev did with his silver foxes, overtime domestication made the dog less dangerous than its wild cousin. Or, it is possible that the less flighty more submissive animals were less frightened to approach human encampments to scavenge on their trash and domestication was a result of this less aggressive gene pool meeting us halfway; as it became more acclimated to human interactions. Either way, domestication did not take as long as once thought. From wolf to *proto dog* to domestic dog; their evolution really happened in a very short amount of time.

Today, all of that has changed. Many domestic dog breeds, as we know them, have only been around since the nineteenth century. The industrial revolution dramatically changed the way human beings lived in Europe. The Victorian era was filled with perfectionists that wanted everything to look and be perfect, including their animals. With this new era, came financial success for many people who often competed for fame or status. Hundreds of dog breeds were created in a very short time by men and women who wanted a pet that could bring them a higher sense of status in the community. They produced their first "lap" dogs. Breeds like the King Charles Cavalier and toy breeds were developed, while ancient breeds like the Shih Tzu and the Pekinese had already long been bred in China.

Then there were the serious hunters that perfected the hunting lines and created dogs like Beagles, Basset Hounds, and the Jack Russell Terrier. The German bred Doberman *Pinscher* was a result of a tax collector's need to have a dog to protect him when collecting taxes, while the herding breeds were also perfected around that time. Now that people could afford the luxury of having a pet; the dog's lifestyle changed dramatically.

We often prefer the easygoing dog that is not driven by its genes of hunting, tracking, or herding for example. Breeds that are genetically hardwired to work are asked to lay around in the living room all day and are scolded for digging up the yard. Beagles end up in shelters by the hundreds because of their "bad behavior" of howling or escaping their environments and exploring the outside world. The problem is nobody told the beagle he wasn't supposed to be a beagle anymore now that he's a pet.

Jack Russell terriers Kiki and Jack get two thirty-minute runs as part of their daily rituals, while Bill looks forward to getting out and enjoying a relaxing scooter ride as well.

Regardless of the breed, every dog needs both physical and mental stimulation, just like we do. Life becomes very boring and unsatisfying when you are limited in your ability to do what comes natural to you. Pent-up energy is the reason why so many dogs are out of control—from the frustrated Jack Russell Terrier, who lives locked up in an apartment, to the Border Collie, who is kept crated for much of the day; these dogs suffer both mentally and physically unless they are well-stimulated and kept tired, so they can enjoy their downtime. *You should have a dog to enjoy, not to annoy.* I believe pets are in our lives to be *stress reducers not stress producers*. But we must allow them to be part of the solution instead of making them just another problem in our lives.

Your dogs' life can't be put on hold for forty hours per week because you're too busy or too tired and only be allowed to flourish on the weekend. I believe that if you cannot take a minimum of *one hour* out of *every twenty-four hours* (more is even better) to spend one-on-one with your pet dog, then you shouldn't have it. Making this commitment is not as hard as you may think. You can break it down to two thirty-minute walks per day and divide this responsibility among your family members or divide it into three twenty-minute sessions throughout the day with your dog, walking it twice for twenty minutes and playing with it in the house or yard the other twenty minutes. Again, you can include family members to help.

The family pet needs to be everyone's responsibility. You should be enjoying your dog *and using this time to retreat from the hectic world you live in* and let this hour a day you put aside for you and your dog be your time to *relax and recharge yourself.* Your dog needs a routine to look forward to and so do you. If your dog is causing you stress, then the chances are your dog feels the same about you. It's a rude awakening, but it's true. Use the time you spend with your dog every day as a stress reducer, and in return, *your dog will repay you* by not being a stress producer.

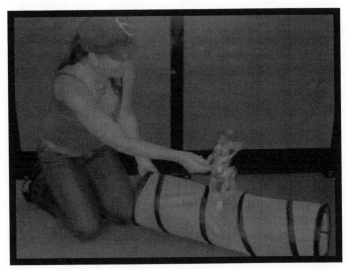

Kaylene keeps her dog Ringo mentally and physically stimulated by teaching him new tricks.

Ringo loves to please Kaylene and loves to show off his skills every chance he gets.

If your dog is a working dog, doing what it was bred to do, then it does not require as much from you mentally or physically because it gets all it needs just by doing what we bred them to do. A ranch dog is perfectly happy in spending its entire life never leaving the ranch or going for a walk in the city or going to the dog park because his needs are fulfilled through his lifestyle. There are dogs such as the Malamute and the Anatolian Shepherd that were bred and hardwired to live outside all their lives doing what they were genetically modified to do. These dogs love it *as long as they are doing their job* because that's who they are. Then we ask them to ignore who they were bred to be, so we can enjoy them as a pet, *living how we want them to live* regardless of what they need to be happy, healthy, and well-balanced dogs.

GOOD PUPPY ACADEMICS

Unfortunately, these dogs always end up on the losing end of the deal. Because often times we don't like what they really are, we just like what they represent.

Learning Theory: The Science of the Mind

Learning theory is a term used to describe the many different aspects of learning in the field of psychology. One of these theories, known as *classical conditioning*, was accidentally discovered by Russian physiologist Ivan Pavlov in 1903 during a lab study in which dogs were being used to measure saliva output during feeding. The food (*unconditioned stimulus*) was used to feed the dog in the experiment and so to measure how much saliva was being produced during the eating and digestive process. As a physiologist, Pavlov was interested *in the body's physical effects*, one that required no learning on the dog's part (*unconditioned response*) to trigger the response. It just had to eat a meal, and the dog's body *automatically* did the rest as part of the digestive process.

In brief, Pavlov noticed that after several repeated sessions, the dogs began anticipating that food was coming (*conditioned stimulus*) and would start salivating automatically (*conditioned response*) before the food was given to them. This physiological reaction was not present when the original experiment started. It became a *conditioned response* induced by the food (*stimulus*). This meant that the dogs *learned* to anticipate, and this was now a *psychological reaction* not simply an *automatic one* as before. So learning just happened naturally. The dog did not have to be taught by anyone to make an association of this kind. It was *nature* that induced this mechanism of learning out of past experiences.

To prove this, Pavlov came up with a controlled way to induce the salivation response without food being introduced. He decided to start ringing a bell prior to introducing the food and found that once the dogs had figured out *the pattern* that food was delivered *after* they heard the bell (*conditioned stimulus*), they would start salivating (*conditioned response*) without food being used. Animal trainers use this exact same method and call it clicker training. Advertising agencies use this strategy by bombarding us with jingles while tempting you with awesome close-up shots of yummy food that makes your mouth water and crave it, so you will buy the product and try it. We are bombarded with classical conditioning every day. We just don't realize it. Mother Nature uses it to teach us *good associations* and *sometimes bad associations*, depending on the situation and lesson to be learned.

This can be seen in the natural world when observing wild wolf behavior. For example, the first time wolf pups are given whole prey to consume, the mother might bring them a small dead animal like a rabbit. At first, the pups see this life-giving food source as satisfying their automatic biological need to feed *(unconditioned response)* as a very pleasant and stimulating activity (positive reinforcement), while new positive neural associations are being formed by the experience. So the pups start looking forward (*conditioned response*) to get a good meal when they see mom hunting and bringing them a delicious rabbit to eat.

The young predators *learn* how to bite, tear, and consume it with a little *stress* from conflicts that erupt between littermates competing for a piece the prize. So their first association of a good meal becomes that of a social event, that is a positive experience (*positive reinforcement*), building the puppy's experience in a confident and motivational way. Then the mother decides to bring a wounded rabbit so the pups can experience a more stressful and challenging situation. Once she is confident that the pups are old enough and capable of handling and killing a wounded rabbit, the mother might bring the pups to a hunt and let them see her down a baby elk. But instead of killing it for the pups, she disables it enough so it cannot get away but can still kick and fight for its life.

This is where the brain game of neurochemistry and psychology merge. It's a field of study known as *cognitive psychology* and was discovered and studied in the 1940s by Swiss developmental psychologist Jean Piaget. It focuses on how childhood experiences are processed, interpreted, and used to help develop new neural pathways. Sensory perception skill and communication skill development, as well as other phases of brain development, are studied in Jean Piaget's *theory of cognitive development.* Jean Piaget did not invent it. He just *discovered, studied, and documented it.* It is definitely something all dog trainers should understand because *it applies to animals as well.*

In his studies, Piaget discovered that *the method in which a new neural pathway is first established* affects the interpretation of the event; thus, our hands-on experiences make us more knowledgeable than just seeing or hearing about it. Piaget calls this the study of *genetic epistemology*, and it focuses on four stages of child development. There are the *sensorimotor, preoperational, concrete operational, and formal operational stages of development* that are focused on learning in the childhood years.

Piaget saw how learning came in stages that he called *assimilation* and *accommodation* to reach the highest levels of learning called *equilibration*, where the brain changes (*neuroplasticity*) its mind (neural pathway) to become more efficient and accurate, adapting to the environment through a sort of trial-and-error fine-tuning mechanism. This transformation is a biological function caused by the learner's experiences and how they initially dealt with a situation. If the experience builds your confidence (positive reinforcement), then you are likely to want to repeat it and continue building up this strong and rewarding pathway. If the first experience is negative, you might be hesitant to continue subjecting yourself to the unpleasant consequences (operant conditioning) and stop using that pathway since it doesn't reward you.

Unlike the harmless rabbit, this little elk has long legs that kick with sharp hooves (+ *positive punishment*), which could *add* an injury or cause pain if they make contact with a pup's face or ribs. This will require the pups to discover new, potentially lifesaving, and survival strategies if they are going to kill and eat this catch. But what if the baby elk somehow escapes with its life, the positive reinforcement of eating it after all that hunting effort will be taken away or *subtracted* (− *negative punishment*), and the pups will not get to eat. By doing this, Mother Nature has built in a method of learning that enables a predator and its prey to make lifesaving, split-second decisions based on both classical conditioning (instinct) that happens to you and is *not consequence based* and operant conditioning that *has consequences* that you learn from. One is like hardware, and the other is like software.

If the mother wolf was to give her pups a live adult elk, which still had some fight left in him, *as their first hunting and feeding experience with an elk,* the pups would freak out or be severely injured if they even got near such an animal. Instinct would drive the pup's new neural pathway to become set as elk representing a life-threatening danger instead of the life-giving food source that they are to the wolf's livelihood. The mother wolf understands that *her young must build up these skills one step at a time* since, as adults, their lives will depend on their ability to take down dangerous elk in a controlled and strategic manner. So it is critical to set up the first learning experience in a way that allows you to build up your knowledge, confidence, and skills efficiently through the learning process (*operant conditioning*) of hands-on experience so that the pups are willing to continue to engage in the learning process by emulating others, problem-solving, as well as through trial and error without becoming too fearful first.

If all this sounds too technical and confusing, *don't let that scare you*. People get degrees in this stuff, so it needs to be labeled, documented, and broken down for our scholarly use. It's how *we* learn. *Nature doesn't work that way. Nature is impulsive yet wise.* In her book, *you are the book,* and you create your own story with every passing moment. Nature is simple. There are limits, and there are boundaries, yet all is in balance in the struggle for survival because *Mother Nature wants everything to live and thrive.* It is the driving force of this entire planet. Even parasites and bacteria have a strong will to live. But mankind likes to think that tinkering with nature, so we can control it, makes us more powerful. Animals don't do that. They are not in a mind-set that enables them to rationalize such irrational things. Only human beings rationalize like that. I think that's what separates us from them.

A famous study done in 1920 by James Watson set out to prove that a person can *learn* to fear something that he never feared before or had no reason to fear by using classical conditioning. The experiment consisted of baby Albert, who was an infant about nine months old at the time, and a white rat. The white rat was introduced to baby Albert in a nice, normal way. Baby Albert liked the white rat and other furry animals as they were first introduced (hardwired) to him as a pleasant experience. Eventually, the same white rat was reintroduced several times accompanied by a loud sound that startled baby Albert and made him afraid of the white rat and other furry animals they introduced to him, proving that outside influences are capable of rewiring the brain (*neuroplasticity*) to interpret a situation differently than it had been hardwired originally.

Watson set out to prove that behavior is learned not genetically set—the opposite of what people like Dmitri

Belyaev advocated. This was the beginning of what's known today as the *behavioral sciences*. It was believed at the time that genetics were what made you who you are, not outside influences. We now know that both genetics (biology) and outside influences (learning) are what make us who we are. And, as Watson proved, some of that can be altered through classical conditioning, because as we now know, *neuroplasticity* allows the brain to change itself.

The mental processes of problem-solving have been studied for over one hundred years by many different scientists. *Cognitive psychology* allows us to appreciate the processes that the brain goes through to learn. *Neuroscience* and *behaviorism* are forms of *cognitive science* that give us the insight we need to better understand how a specific organism processes information and uses it to benefit from it. A much needed skill if you are to survive everyday adversities. Problem-solving requires some trial and error and lots of creativity and perseverance. *Nature gave animals these abilities so they can figure all this survival stuff out*, and we can use it for our benefit.

For example, if a dog was lost in the woods and started getting hungry, his brain would get him sniffing around to find some calories. All the body cares about is getting the proteins and carbohydrates it needs to keep the brain happy so it can continue keeping our vital systems running at top efficiency. *The animal becomes the servant of this mechanism*. The dog's nose suddenly picks up the scent of a big, fat grub, full of life-giving nutrients, but it is stuck in a deep crevice in the log. The brain tells the dog that it better seize this opportunity and figure out how to get that meal, so the dog tries biting at the log.

When that strategy fails to produce results, the dog changes its strategy and starts digging and clawing at the log, then barks at the log, trying every move possible, but all this effort goes unrewarded, starting to make that grub less appealing since now the dog has expending more calories, trying to get the grub, than the meal has to offer. Finally, he lies down to rethink the situation and to give himself a rest from the stress that problem-solving caused. In nature, the gambler must know when to continue and when to fold. In psychology, this form of learning is understood as *operant conditioning*.

Theorized by behavioral psychologist B. F. Skinner in the 1920s, *operant conditioning* is a consequence-based method of learning. Unlike classical conditioning which occurs involuntarily, voluntary behavior modification is the key to this form of learning. The animal adjusts its behavior to manipulate the outcome of the situation at hand with the hopes of gaining reward or pleasure from his successful actions versus becoming more uncomfortable and less successful, being left consequently unrewarded, by all this hard work. So behavior gets conditioned by how it was learned through environmental consequence caused by your direct interaction with an experience. Sometimes you're rewarded for your creative efforts, and sometimes you're not; if your attempts don't produce positive results, it's the *"you've got to live it to learn it"* school of hard knocks at times, but that's *nature's way*, and we can't change it. We can only benefit from it.

In the natural world, it does not take an animal weeks or months to learn basic skills when it comes to eating and staying alive. From birth on, every opportunity that presents itself as a challenge must be dealt with in the moment and remembered for future recall when needed in high stress situations like hunger or danger. It may take baby predators a couple of years to learn how to kill a large animal efficiently, but he gets to that point by learning another piece of the strategy every time he hunts. Predator's success rate at catching a good meal is not very high. Predators do not succeed at making the kill every time they hunt. Remember, the animals that predators eat don't want to be eaten! They have their survival strategies as well. In psychology, this is known *as intermittent reinforcement,* and it is a powerful influence in Mother Nature's survival scheme. Gambling houses and lotteries capitalize on this principle to run a successful business. And we are attracted to it because it's encoded in our genes.

Knowing how this works in the natural world, I utilize this concept when teaching dogs and puppies how to lie down. I learned this from Bonnie Bergin. Starting from having the dog or puppy in the standing position, you use a high-value treat like real chicken (the grub) to capture the dog's nose (scent). With your palm facing the floor, draw the treat *straight down* from the nose to the floor. Be sure the dog can't get the treat from your hand (the log) but do allow it to sniff and take a great interest in it. Here is where *marking the behavior* is critical if you are to quickly teach this lesson and set the new neural pathways. Using a *clicker* or the word *yes* to mark a behavior, tells the dog's brain when it has done something right and is being rewarded for succeeding. Remember the brain game and those pathways through the grass? Well, this is it. This is where *the neuroscience kicks in.* You are now setting those first pathways.

Providing the dog or puppy is food motivated, you will actually see the animal problem-solving the way, which I described it above with the grub in a log. Here is what I call the "three's a charm rule." The first time the dog or puppy lies down successfully to your cues, and you mark the behavior and deliver the high-value reward immediately. The victory is recorded by the brain as nothing more than a successful maneuver; therefore, the dog should be influenced to repeat it next time it encounters this situation. When you immediately repeat the behavior and succeed again, the dog's brain records it as a sort of *Déjà vu* moment the second time and now predicts how his actions will affect the outcome, so he repeats what he did the last time to succeed. The third time in a row the dog tries to lie down and succeeds; the brain sees it as a predictable pattern and should now be able to do it again the fourth time without problem-solving. Learning something new, like lying down, really can be taught that quickly. Because in the natural world, the faster you learn the more frequently you will eat, and nature often rewards us for our creativity in achieving success. *It's the no skill no kill rule,* and we all live by it.

In psychology, there is a theory called *tabula rasa* also known *as the blank slate*. This idea, interestingly enough, goes way back to ancient psychology books Aristotle wrote. It states that you come into this life with no built-in experiences in your head and no perception of anything. From the moment you are born, every life experience (nurture) you have programs you, developing your personality and intelligence, perceiving information and storing it for future recall.

This is how we learn new things. The way a neural pathway is first set becomes the initial foundation of the animal's experience toward that situation. *The memory* of how you felt in a given situation (pain or pleasure) is chemically stored for future recall, just waiting to become activated to cross that electric neural pathway (synapsis) again and trigger a response according to your interpretation and perception of that situation during past experiences. This favors the nurture theory that states that our personality, intelligence, and social behaviors are learned and nurtured rather than set at birth.

Patterns and Rituals

Ever wonder how some of these wildlife moviemakers and photographers get the shots they get? Sometimes, it's luck. But you can't depend on luck when you have a project with a deadline and a budget. So knowing the habits of whatever animal you are trying to capture on film allows these professionals the ability to predict that certain behaviors are likely to occur at certain times. They can be reasonably sure that they will get the footage they seek based on what they have observed the animal doing in the recent past. That is because animals, including us, *all* live in some rhythm of patterns and rituals. Whales gather to breed at certain times in certain waters. Bears fish for salmon when the salmon are running. So filmmakers take advantage of these patterns and rituals to get the footage they need.

So what does any of this have to do with training a domestic dog or puppy? Well, like these filmmakers, there are many ways you can use this strategy because your domesticated canine will also seek to have patterns and rituals in its daily routine. These patterns and rituals will either be set in their brain *to accommodate you* through your training efforts, or they will set themselves to accommodate your dog. I suggest *you* to set these patterns and rituals before your dog does. Dogs that set their own neural pathways, causing inappropriate patterns and rituals, end up in shelters, and many get euthanized. All because their natural tendencies to repeat behaviors that we find undesirable was never redirected, curbed, or eliminated by the humans who are responsible for training them.

This is why I mentioned before that if you cannot give your dog *at least* one hour (more is better) out of every twenty-four hours of your day, you shouldn't have a dog as a pet. Your dog *needs* to have *healthy* rituals and patterns built into its life to practice every single day. These healthy patterns allow your dog to enjoy its downtime because it knows that it is guaranteed appropriate stimulation two or three times a day. Dogs whose neural pathways are set to good patterns are happier, healthier, and mentally stable pets because these productive, balanced rhythms are recognized in their genes.

Dogs have been known to bring you their leash or bring you your shoes around the time they know you're supposed to take them on their ritual walk. It's what dogs do. It comes natural for them to know when these times are. If we honor this rhythm within them, we will enjoy the feedback we get from our pets. If we choose to ignore or stifle it, we will not enjoy the feedback we get from our dogs because they will feel out of sync and unfulfilled, causing *instability* in the dog's psyche, manifesting itself into some (or all) of the following behaviors: *howling, digging, escaping, running away, destroying the house or yard, withdrawn, neurotic pacing, housebreaking issues, obsessive licking, aggression, fearfulness, being anxious, jumping, biting, nipping, disobeying your authority, marking territory*, and so on. All the behaviors that are programmed in the 99.8 percent of the wolf genes, that we have not altered, will manifest and become magnified *as nature takes over and sets those neural pathways for you.*

That is why it is so important for you to set them yourself and continue to use them to keep the overgrowth (nature) that is waiting dormant from reawakening and reclaiming (overgrowth) the pathway again. Make sense? It is really very basic and simple. But you must put in the effort it takes to teach and lead your canine student consistently. They will not change their behaviors themselves. They have no idea what you expect from them unless you teach them. You are the source of their behavior.

But are these really *instabilities* in a dog? They aren't if you are a Farrell dog or wolf. They are Mother Nature's survival techniques for the canine species. We call these behaviors unstable because we are asking these animals to tone it down and be more like us to fit into our societies safely and not to annoy others around us as well. It's the same etiquette we expect from our own and from other people's children in public. It's what gives our society the structure needed for everyone to live in harmony and be productive and treated fairly. No society should be expected to put up with any unruly adult, adolescent, child, or animal. And society won't. That's why it is critical to teach our pets and our own young the etiquette they need to fit in and succeed in the society that they reside in.

At least, we and our kids have choices. We can choose to say, "I won't live by these rules" and go off and do our thing, knowing what the consequences are to our actions. One might take the productive stance and go live in a remote area to avoid their conflicts of interests. Or one might take the rebel path and end up in the prison system for noncompliance to social etiquette. *A dog doesn't have this option.* It is stuck with what you provide for it. That's why you shouldn't even consider owning a dog as a pet if you are not going to train it to be an acceptable part of society. It's just not fair to the dog. In fact, poor social etiquette becomes an infraction worthy of the death sentence for many pet dogs. Mother Nature doesn't cause these ills. We do.

Think of everything your dog does consistently as a pattern the dog has been either preconditioned to automatically do because of its biology (hardware), training, or out of habit (software). When you find yourself delighted with your dog's consistent behaviors, think of those as desired patterns or programs. When you find yourself annoyed with a consistent behavior, think of it as nothing more than an undesired pattern or program. *Behaviors that are consistent are just patterns.* Some are good, and some are not. You are responsible for whatever behaviors you allow your dog to continue practicing.

Spending 100 percent of your time and effort in practicing good patterns with your dog will save you from spending 100 percent of your frustration and time on correcting your dog, for spending 100 percent of his time practicing the patterns *you have allowed him to set*. Knowing your dog's patterns is important since your dog will definitely be observing yours.

It's an animal's *nature* to know the patterns and rituals of the animals that live in their environment. For example, some dogs start getting anxious right before you leave for work as they see the routine of you getting ready and anticipate being left home alone.

My dog, on the other hand, can't wait for me to go to work and even brings me my shoes without being asked just to hurry the process because I have conditioned him that the pattern of me leaving for work means that he will get to have his favorite, treat stuffed, interactive toy right before I step out and leave. It has become part of the ritual that I intentionally set so that I could control his interpretation (program) of what me leaving for work means to him. Sometimes, (intermittently), I'll even hide a few extra treats for him to find in the room, just to keep him guessing and interested, since he can never predict my pattern of when or where he might find something extra that week.

CHAPTER 2

Why I Don't Train That Way

MOST OF US are familiar with the movie *Mary Poppins*. When I think of the two different strategies used to parent the children in the story, it reminds me of *why I don't train that way*. In the story, the children's father has a ridged disciplinary style. His children react in his presents with military precision. They are well-behaved and attentive to their father's every word. They are well-cared for and loved, yet they don't have a sense of confidence about them and never have a smile on their faces. The children look good on the outside but are suffering silently on the inside. Unable to express themselves as the creative intelligent children they really are. What's wrong with this picture is that the emphasis on the children's behavior was focused on how the father wanted his children to *represent him* instead of how they should learn to represent *themselves*.

Then Mary Poppins is hired as the children's nanny. Her style of communication with the children is also firm, and there is no doubt that she is in charge. But Mary Poppins makes the children smile when she disciplines them. By building up their confidence, she brings out their natural ability to problem-solve and express themselves and be active-willing participants in the process. The children are still well-behaved, yet they have a much more relaxed and natural demeanor about them. Mary Poppins understood how to bring out the best in these children and did it in a fun, structured, and natural way. In the movie, Mary Poppins' talents were portrayed as magic, and it really is when you see how you can make things happen *by working with Mother Nature instead of against it.*

I want to tap into this "magic" resource as well, so my subjects can be active, willing, and confident participants who enjoy my guidance and find it naturally rewarding to cooperate. Knowing my leadership is sensible, stable, and fair, triggering a less stressful endorphin or "feel-good" neurotransmitter response in the learning process, since positive reinforcement is already recognized in their genes instead of them having an unhealthy, high stress, adrenaline response that heightens their fight, flight, or avoidance response, as this too is recognized in their genes.

Knowing what I know about neuroscience, psychology, and learning keeps me from using negative reinforcement to teach my subjects. But is there a place for negative reinforcement in nature? Let's think about that. In psychology, negative reinforcement is defined as something unpleasant that keeps up its intensity until *you do something* to change the situation and make the unpleasant consequence stop.

I believe that in the natural world, negative reinforcement is used as a life-or-death mechanism. It is Mother Nature's last resort and is used to promote healthy life-giving habits. I think the basic need for food, water, and shelter tops the list for how Mother Nature uses negative reinforcement. From the day animals are born, their bodies automatically alert them when they are thirsty, hungry, hot, or cold. This also applies to human beings as the need to feed and find shelter is the primitive component of nature we share with all living things. If you don't heed the call and satisfy these needs, you will become physically uncomfortable with hunger pains and dry mouth. Same holds true if you are caught out in the heat or in the cold.

If you do not eat, drink, and find shelter, Mother Nature will not be able to help you thrive because in the natural world, the consequence to not responding to the discomfort (negative reinforcement) that hunger, thirst, and lack of proper shelter brings will eventually cause death. This form of negative reinforcement is biological (hardware), and there is no way around it. It is designed to make living things have to participate and work to survive. There is no free ride in the natural world. Mother Nature is your partner, not your servant.

Another way I see Mother Nature using negative reinforcement is during mating and territory disputes. Many animals fight to the death to protect their best interests. Killing your competition allows your dominant genetic line a better chance at survival. But many animals *choose* not to let a situation become life-threatening and will surrender or flee and let the spoils go to the more superior animal to avoid life-threatening injury. Every living thing on earth is here for one purpose, to live and reproduce another day. If you are dead, you can't do that, so living with a survival strategy is the norm in the natural world. Even slight injuries can lead to infection and death, so *animals use their ability to choose* their consequence wisely to live and thrive as long as possible.

Bears are a great example of how this phenomena plays out in the wild. Every year in America, certain streams and rivers become filled with Salomon, swimming upstream from the ocean back to their birth place to reproduce and die. Bears are solitary animals that usually come together only to breed. They are not pack-oriented animals like dogs are. Yet every year when the streams and rivers fill with Salmon, hundreds of bears (some with cubs) gather together to harvest their share of the bounty. Without the Salomon in their diet, these bears would all have to work twice as hard to get the awesome nourishment provided by this overly abundant, high fat, easy-to-catch fish. And since these bears are so preoccupied with catching and eating this easy prey, the other animals they usually prey on get a break from being eaten by bears!

These bears often get into territorial spats since there is such a high concentration of them hunting in the same small area. Fighting to the death in these situations is rare as the whole point of being there is to take advantage of this bountiful harvest. Their genes know that there is no reason to die over such an abundance of resources. This is Mother Nature's switch, so to speak, so everyone has an equal opportunity to choose their own consequences. Positive reinforcement is now the method the bears are experiencing. In psychology, positive reinforcement means that you are rewarded for making choices that allow you to continue experiencing pleasurable consequences instead of unpleasant ones. Dying or fighting over one fish when there is plenty for everyone is a poor survival strategy in Mother Nature's book.

Positive reinforcement has its consequences as well, but unlike negative reinforcement that keeps up its intensity and causes stress, Mother Nature uses what's known in psychology as positive punishment, because you are *adding* (+) an unpleasant consequence, and negative punishment, because you are *subtracting* (−) something pleasant the animal wanted. Giving the animal a chance to learn from its choices in a less stressful, threatening way where there is always a reward involved if you learn your lessons and heed all of Mother Nature's signals. Canines are predators. Predators eat things that don't want to be eaten. Animals such as skunks and porcupines have a defense that serves as a warning to help detour the predator from eating it.

The porcupine will stomp its feet and make noise to try intimidating the predator into leaving it alone. When that doesn't work, they spread out their quills and run backward toward the predator embedding very sharp spikes called quills into their face or their bodies that *add* (+) an unpleasant consequence (*positive punishment*), meant as a warning to save themselves from getting eaten; this gives the predator a chance to rethink his strategy. The predator must now make a choice as to whether the *painful quills* (+ positive punishment) are worth the consequence of *not eating* (− negative punishment). If the predator was to decide that it's worth the gamble and gets poked by a sharp quill, he has to reassess the situation as to whether or not *he chooses* (operant conditioning) to continue subjecting himself to this unpleasant experience. If he walks away now, he could starve. But if he makes the wrong move and gets a whole face full of painful quills that embed and get infected, he will not be able to hunt, and hunger (negative reinforcement) will eventually kill him.

So now the predator's nature says survival is the norm. Change your strategy, and don't keep trying to eat porcupines. Spend your time and energy looking for those rabbits whose only defense is outrunning and outsmarting the predator. The only consequence the predator has when hunting rabbit is in not catching it. But he gets to live another day to try again. Even large prey like deer uses positive punishment to keep predators from eating them. They use their sharp antlers and hooves to try and convince the predator (operant conditioning) to think again and detour his efforts, so he gets the chance to win the gamble of not getting eaten.

The animals that are the best at using positive punishment effectively live the longest because it is an important skill to have. Deer will also use negative reinforcement by relentlessly lunging at their opponent with both front legs and using their sharp hoofs in an attempt to kill it or convince the predator to flee with its life. It's either fight or flight, and both predator and prey live by this standard. Flight could cost you your life as could fight. Either way, it's always a gamble you hope to win.

Wolf in submission. *Olga Mirenska/Dreamstime.com*

Being overly assertive and forcing your dog into giving you a behavior through negative reinforcement and intimidation taps into the *adult wolf's* mentality. Adult wolves often treat adolescent and other adult family members aggressively and harshly to keep them submissive in order to maintain a balance of authority within individual ranks, but puppies are not treated that way when they are young. Adult wolves *adore* their puppies, indulging them with affection and food, while exhibiting patience and self-control to communicate *on the puppy's level* since the puppy's innate high-pitched vocals and appeasement behaviors trigger a submission response in the rest of the pack toward them. This is Mother Nature's way of setting the first neural pathways in a positive and constructive manner. Adults don't expect their young to rise to their level until they are older and have accumulated some skills to perfect.

A wolf mother and her pup enjoying a rest in the morning sun. Wolves adore their young, lavishing them with affection. *Designpicssub/Dreamstime.com*

Our domestic dogs are not a danger to us because we retarded their mental and physical traits through eugenic experimentation that capitalized on accentuating those genetic puppy traits found in the wolf's young. Known as neoteny, we wanted our pet's mentality to remain more like puppies for the rest of their adult lives since puppies don't kill and want to appease their superiors who keep them safe, feed, and teach them rewarding skills. So we bred them for these traits.

Some dogs are more neotenized than others. A German Shepherd dog is not as neotenized as a beagle, for example. You can see the adult wolf in the German Shepherd dog's physical appearance and in its behaviors as adults when compared to the beagle that doesn't look or act anything like an adult wolf. Remember, in the past, those domestic dogs that were too aggressive to do their jobs where seen as a danger and burden and would likely be eliminated from the gene pool to insure the domestic dog's survival as man's best friend, as it is believed that the wolf was the first animal domesticated by man.

For the adult wolf, aggression and a sharp fight or flight and avoidance response is how you stay safe, balanced, and alive. Have you ever wondered why the African zebra or the African wild dog was never domesticated and used for man's advancement with the native people like the horse and the wolf were? It's because in Africa, there are so many different predators that want to eat you and these fight, flight, and aggression reactions are your only tools for survival, which means these animals *are genetically super hardwired* to be mean, nasty, and to never submit to any predator including man.

Wild dogs of Africa are so skilled at killing that a pack of thirty or more dogs can take down three large animals at a time during the same hunt out of one herd. Something wolves don't do. They are driven by the neurochemical adrenaline that makes them very aggressive and highly skilled as hunters but not safe to handle by humans. These wild dogs have the highest success rate in the hunt compared to other predators. They truly are precise killing machines. And they owe it all to their biochemistry.

Zebra may look like horses, but their temperament makes them too hard to domesticate. *Davidcrehner/ Dreamstime.com*

Domestic horse. *Dizajune/Dreamstime.com*

A pack of African wild dogs tries to eliminate a rival predator. These wild dogs are highly skilled killing machines. *Mogens Trolle/Dreamstime.com*

Gray Wolf. *James Hearn/Dreamstime.com*

The wolf and the horse, on the other hand, live in less harsh environments with a lot more resources and less aggressive prey animals to sustain them, as well as less large predators to compete with. When animals don't have to be as assertive and nasty to survive, their adrenaline response is more manageable than the animals living in high stress environments like Africa, where the struggle for life and death is much more competitive and challenging. The same biochemical reaction can surface in the domestic dog if it is forced to live in a high stress fight or flight state of mind by people or other animals that threaten or abuse them.

Man's earliest settlements in the Middle East were only possible with the domestication of the dog and other animals like the donkey, cat, sheep, goat, pig, cattle, and camel, helping feed and farm human developments. Without them, mankind would still be depending on hunting, gathering, and traveling with the animals they hunt for a living. There are not very many animals on the planet that are either grass eaters (prey) or meat eaters (predators) that man has been able to domesticate enough to utilize safely, and the domestic dog made it possible for us to keep large flocks and herds of these animals. Without the dog, we could never have kept sheep and cattle under control or safe from predators once we domesticated them; dogs gave man the edge in every aspect of his modern development and continue doing so till today.

Training an animal from the inside out rather than from the outside in requires you to know how that animal sees the world and learns from it. It's like working with a two- or three-year-old human child. They live in a different reality in their own heads because they are incapable at that age to think any differently. Training a dog should be about them, not about you. Your dog can't think like you. He is not human. He thinks like the canine species that he is.

You must learn to think like a dog and influence him in a way that his genes recognize. Knowing how he learns is the key to understanding and utilizing nature's way. If you are tapping into the wrong neurochemicals, you will not get the results you are hoping for. You want to use positive reinforcement, positive punishment, and negative punishment to activate and influence 0.2 percent of *the wolf-puppy part of your dog's brain chemicals* when training it, not the 99.8 percent of the adult-wolf part that you tap into when you use aggression and human will to control your canine subject.

Just like in a wild wolf pack, there are some dogs that need more physical intervention and discipline than others depending on their individual personality traits and talents. If we were all the same, we wouldn't need each other. That's why Mother Nature has given us such a variety of intelligence and abilities within the same species. We need the brave ones who are willing to take risks and lead or protect others as well as hunt if we are to survive. And we also need the ones who are willing to follow and assist the leaders to ensure the livelihood of their offspring who make up the next generation.

Not everyone is suited to do the same thing—that's Mother Nature's design. It takes teamwork from extroverts and introverts, leaders and followers, to run a balanced society.

So before getting a new dog or puppy, find out what type of personality traits you possess, first, and then pick your pet based on those traits over all their other traits, such as specific look, gender, or size. It's about what's inside your dog that's important. Not it's outer appearance or even its standard for that specific breed. Just like with us, each dog's temperament and personality makes them who they are—unique individuals.

Beautiful Roxy, a whippet Shepherd mix, has a unique look. Mixed breeds are often one of a kind since the canine's genes can be arranged to produce many varieties in their species.

Bonnie Bergin's service dog training methods and how to match the right dog with the right person is the most humane and sensible way to train and choose *any dog*, not just service dogs, because *she didn't invent it. Mother Nature did.* Bonnie just utilized nature to succeed the same way she did with her human subjects. Integrating dog psychology and what she knew about our own psychology enabled her to eventually find the right balance needed to train a dog efficiently and effectively. After all, by studying nonhuman animals, early behavioral psychologists had identified the basic procedures that are important in human learning as well. We learned this science from the animals to begin with. It only makes sense to use it on them too.

Choosing the Right Dog

Training your dog is only part of what makes them better pets and companions. Choosing a dog that *suits your needs and lifestyle* is the key to having a pleasant, fulfilling, lifelong relationship with your pet dog. Although it is tempting to choose the dog or puppy that is cute or the one that picks you, this often proves to be the worst way to choose your pet. If you choose an animal due to a spontaneous emotional response, it might end up being more than you bargained for.

Pug Fuji and his American Bulldog housemate Kong enjoying some relaxing together time.

After years of training and placing the first service dog teams, Bonnie Bergin realized that the dog and the handler had to be more alike than different for the teams to last and work together without stress or conflict. The match had to be perfect to work. So Bonnie turned to a method she had discovered at an event. It's called *Wilson's Learning* "social styles," which is used by business people that want to capitalize on the different social styles people have to offer by giving them those tasks that best suit their natural tendencies and individual personalities. Bonnie eventually discovered that by simply matching the right personality types and making sure the dog was always a little less assertive than his partner proved to be the most successful way to match a service dog with a disabled individual.

This strategy can work to your benefit when choosing the right dog or puppy to share your life with. For example, if you are an introvert, don't get an extrovert personality dog. If you are not that outgoing and don't like social interactions, don't get a dog that thrives on being outgoing and social unless you plan on changing *your* social style, and avoid high-energy dogs if you are not willing to be active with it because you are not going to convince a dog to change his social style that easily. If you try, you will be inhibiting the dog's natural tendencies and cause it to become frustrated. This is when undesired behavioral issues can emerge. There is a right dog for everyone out there as they are as individual as we are. You just have to know what you are looking for before choosing and assessing a new dog or puppy's personality traits.

Before getting any dog do your research. Get to know what different breeds were bred to do—hounds track things, terriers chase and catch things, and shepherd dogs protect and herd things, and so on. If you want a dog that's not a hunter, tracker, or herder, choose a breed that was designed to be a lap dog like a King Charles spaniel or a Papillion, for example.

For large breeds, the Saint Bernard or the Newfoundland can make great "giant" lap dogs. But keep in mind that whether large or small, even a lap dog needs proper exercise and mental stimulation that gives them the opportunity to problem-solve and participate in healthy daily patterns and rituals set by you. Obedience training helps you to exercise their mind on behaviors (neural pathways) *you create* to keep them stable and more predictable.

Lillie loves to dress up while Rico prefers the natural look. Both enjoy being pampered, but we must be careful to not spoil them.

So even if you do find the perfect match for you, training the dog or puppy needs to be part of the relationship you build on with your new canine family member. Since even the perfect dog has 99.8 percent wolf embedded in its genes waiting to be activated by the environment (operant conditioning) or through its biology (classical conditioning), so you must exercise the 0.2 percent of the dog that we have domesticated to control and override the 99.8 percent wild within them. This makes you a responsible canine guardian, as we only "own" our dogs according to the laws of man, since someone has to take legal responsibility for a dog's actions if we are to keep them as safe pets in our human society. We are simply their guardians, however, according to the laws of Mother Nature.

Before choosing a dog, ask yourself what purpose your dog will serve. If you're active, have endurance, and like exploring the great outdoors, be sure and get a dog that can accommodate you. A Husky would love that, an English bulldog, not so much. If you are limited in your mobility, then get a slower moving dog with calmer energy, and so on. *Match your personality and energy level with a dog that best suits you.*

When choosing the right dog or puppy, being able to predict temperament is not easy. There are no guarantees that you will be able to predict future behavior based solely on how a puppy or dog seems to be a certain age. There are things, however, that you can observe when trying to find a dog or puppy that's *right for you*. Body language, tail carriage, and ear movements can often give you clues to some of a dog's personality traits. If a dog is a bad match regardless of how cute it is and how much you love it, there will always be stress involved in the relationship. Dogs are as varied as we are when it comes down to temperament. Some people are passive, some people are assertive, and some people are even downright mean. You will find the same in the animal world.

Dogs are very similar to us in certain ways. In fact, all mammals are *basically* the same inside. We all have a heart, lungs, skeleton, and so on, in all about the same places. Depending on how you stand or are built will determine where those things are located. So take a close look at your dog. If you could see his skeleton and everything inside of him and you stood him upright on his back legs, you will see what I mean.

Look at your dog's feet. Did you know they walk on their toes? Think about your dog's vocalizations. Low drawn out vocalizations, such as a growl, and high-pitched barking convey two different messages. If I speak to you in a stern, low tone, the message is very clear. If I speak to you in the soft, sweet high-pitched tone, the same is true. However, your dog is also very different than you. They do not see or interpret the world the same. They do not rationalize before they react. They only rationalize when they are problem-solving.

Finding the Right Trainer

Bonnie Bergin wasn't the only dog trainer using positive reinforcement methods in the 1970s. Many trainers were practicing operant and classical conditioning. People such as Hollywood animal trainers had been using it for many years. Famous dogs on television like Lassie and Benji had to be trained humanly because of the laws protecting animal actors. Everyone knows and loves Eddie, the Jack Russell Terrier that was on the Fraser TV show. Do you think pinch collars and negative reinforcement is how he was trained? Wouldn't you think that would be unfair to exploit him that way?

Eddie, whose real name is Moose, loved his work because it fulfilled his innate need to problem-solve and work for a living, while his efforts were rewarded nature's way. It had become his duty to go to work and have a purpose. Positive reinforcement is the reason this Jack Russell Terrier, and his human counterparts, performed with such confidence and enthusiasm. Simply put, the pay was good, and the work was challenging yet enjoyable. The latest talented Jack Russell Terrier that we admire today is Uggy, who was recently in the movie *The Artist* and was also trained this way.

Like other animal trainers, Bonnie Bergin found that by using positive reinforcement methods with her canine students, she could produce a dog that would exhibit automatic behaviors without always having to be told what to do; because like our Jack Russell friend Eddie, dogs love to repeat patterns and rituals that reward them. He learned many patterns on that set that he did over and over again every week, like staring at Frasier, holding a down stay while on the couch for long periods of time, and running to the back room when he was done with his scene. Over the years, these behaviors became almost automatic since he knew the pattern he was expected to repeat over and over every episode.

Not all, but many dog trainers use a mentality geared toward "mastering the beast," so to speak, because they are following old traditions that are very out-of-date and set by working people who dominated their animals physically because they knew nothing about psychology, concentrating on the pain instead of the pleasure method to train their dogs.

Some hunting dogs are taught to have a soft mouth with decoys that have nail-like prongs poking out so the dog feels pain in its tender mouth when biting down, or using what's known as the ear pinch to teach the hunting dog to drop the bird on command through negative reinforcement, service dogs are taught the same thing when retrieving your sunglasses or dropping an item onto your lap, but like the entertainment dogs we so admire, like Moose and Uggy, positive reinforcement or pleasure was used to teach Bonnie Bergin's service dogs these skills instead of using pain to provoke their cooperation. It's really not necessary to teach a dog by intimidating them to cooperate. It shows a leader's weakness, *the way I (and the dog) see it.*

Dolphins are great problem-solvers. Mother Nature often rewards creativity, so dolphin trainers capitalize on this to teach them new behaviors. *Pdiaz/Dreamstime.com*

Because these animals are not domesticated, tropical birds, dolphins, wolves, and rats can't be forced to submit to human will like a dog can. *Hwee Fuan Tey/ Dreamstime.com*

Kiki loves practicing agility. Positive reinforcement must be used to train these behaviors. Using human will and negative reinforcement is not necessary or effective.

Neuroscience and the field of psychology have finally seriously merged and caught up with what many animal trainers and Bonnie Bergin have been doing for decades with their subjects. In fact, neuroscience is finally being used and recognized as a new way to help people with mental health issues caused by chemical imbalances in the brain. It's not new science but rather old theories that can now be measured and analyzed with our advances in technology.

In addition, Bonnie was using interspecies communication skills (dog psychology) that she learned along the way to motivate, understand, and converse with her canine students. Today, we have horse, dog, and everything else whisperers, but because Bonnie Bergin was so ahead of her time *with the service dog concept*, most people thought her dog whispering was nuts back then.

Finding a qualified dog trainer who understands the brain game and uses operant and classical conditioning *as the foundation of their training* is important. If you can train another species of animal, such as a rat, cat, dolphin, or bird, for example, using the same positive reinforcement strategies you are using to teach your dog, then you are choosing the best way. Negative reinforcement is not the answer. You can't force human will or use harsh discipline or intimidation to teach these animals a new skill. But with operant and classical conditioning, you can teach any animal skills, providing it is within the range of their ability because *they will decide* the consequence *and adjust their needs to suit yours* in order to gain access to the reward, because it's encoded in their genes.

Rats, cats, dolphins, and birds are obviously different than dogs in how they think and what motivates them. But regardless of the animal's species, the right way to train is always the humane way. Learning is a process. Taking shortcuts to get faster results will eventually work against you because what you put into your dog is what you are going to get back out of your dog. Some things take longer to learn than others. Be patient and consistent, you will eventually see results once the new pattern (neural pathway) gets more and more embedded with every use, eventually overriding the old software (program).

You can't have an "alpha" mind-set either. You need to have a confident leader mind-set that encourages and motivates your subjects into wanting to cooperate because doing so *fulfills something within them*. This will make *them choose you* as their alpha in a confident, influential way, not in a forced, fearful, or negative way. If you set the neural pathways in a negative way, the dog will experience chemical synapses that say, "You better do as your leader says, or you might be rejected and punished." *This is the adult-wolf survival mentality.* You want the domestic dog mentality to mimic the *wolf puppy's mentality* whose chemical signals say to "cooperate with your mentors and learn from them because it's always safer and rewarding to follow their lead" since the adults make decisions based on the best interests of your survival.

Malamute Luka watches while puppy Bella and terrier mix Sparky engage in play. *Photo by: Julie Aitken.*

That's what you get when you set the neural pathways in a positive way, so those pathways are set to see your leadership as more of a confident alpha who protects you instead of rejects you. Respect can be forced or natural; if you are *forced* to respect someone, then *that's not natural*. Respect for your leadership is something that must be earned through experience, teamwork, and trust. Puppies should begin training as soon as possible as new neuroassociations are being set on their blank slate the day they are born. The first sixteen weeks of a domestic puppy's life, the window of socialization, is genetically set for them to learn (set new neural pathways) about their surroundings and how they should interact with people, pets, and in new places. At sixteen weeks of age, this gene turns off. For a wolf puppy, this gene shuts off at fourteen weeks.

The study of *Epigenetics* has shown us that, depending on nurture or nature, our genes are constantly being turned on and off. So the brain can alter a genes expression depending on environmental or genetic stimulation by enabling or disabling it. So if a dog associates socializing as a fearful, dangerous or highly stressful event the experience can actually change the brains neural structure the same way good, stimulation and safe associations can. So you must program this in favor of the genes you wish to activate and strengthen.

A canine's life span is so much shorter than ours that they must learn everything they need to know about survival the first two years of their lives and then just keep maintaining it and getting better at it until they die. If you are a wolf puppy, you are very vulnerable and have to be careful not to get eaten yourself. So mother wolves and the rest of the pack teach their young from the moment they leave the den what to *stay away from* and who *not to* socialize with since your own gene pool (pack) are the only animals you are permitted to be social with. In the wild, you are either hunting or being hunted. You must know when to fight and when to flight. These are some of the most important rules to live by if you are going to beat the odds and live to reach the age of two.

With our domestic puppies, *we teach them the opposite* since they are not hunter nor hunted. We concentrate more on socializing them with a lot of different people and other animals that are not family members. *We don't concentrate on developing their fight and flight responses like the wolves do with their young.* This is where the 0.2 percent of domesticated dog separates them from their wild cousins. We choose the most social and less frightened pups (gene pool) from the wolf, which is a death sentence for a wolf pup in the wild, and capitalized on it to create our domestic dog.

Our domestic dogs are really wolves that never grew out of the juvenile stage of development. In the field of *developmental biology,* this phenomenon is called *pedomorphism* or *neoteny,* which means that juvenile traits are retained even after the animal reaches adulthood. In other words, you never grow up. It's what occurred in the Russian silver fox study. Our domestic dogs need to remain puppy like to avoid the danger of them reverting back to the dangerous predator that some of them can become.

They must also be exposed to *our world* in a socially different way than a wolf puppy because they have to live among us and other animals in a peaceful, nonpredation way. We feed them their meals so they have no need to kill for a living. But we still need to repress their innate predatory drives and remind them not to act like hunters sometimes as cats and other small furry things, as well as our own children, occupy the same territories as our pet dogs.

Dogs and cats can live together peacefully, but some dogs need more supervision and training than others to control their impulse to chase.

Safety concerns about disease are warranted. So you must be very careful how and where you expose your puppy to minimize the risk of illness. Veterinarians will warn you that your puppy should never leave the house before it has received its full series of shots. Unfortunately, the puppy will already be at least four to five months old before this occurs.

What most veterinarians fail to tell people is that they could be bringing home diseases on their shoes and hands without ever knowing it, making their puppy ill, even though it's never left the house. I often hear people say, "We leave the puppy at home and take the other dogs to the dog park." If the Parvo virus was present on the ground in that park, you can be bringing it home on your shoes or on your dog's feet and then depositing it in your environment where your puppy can now be exposed.

Reputable breeders who spend a lot of money investing in their puppies are very careful about exposing them to this type of danger. They will usually have you wash your hands and either take off your shoes or step into a bleach solution prior to entering any space the puppies will be exposed to. Parvo is a horrible disease. It is a very tiny virus that can remain dormant and deadly in the soil for up to a year. If you just moved into a new home and the last tenant's dog had Parvo, your puppy can catch it from your own yard, without you ever knowing where it came from. Airborne viruses like distemper and the corona virus are also dangerous and can be deadly as well, so you must be careful.

So now what? How do you train your puppy, before it is fully vaccinated, very carefully? Puppies are given a series of four different rounds of shots before they are five months old. Ideally, by six to seven weeks of age, your puppy should have received its first set. The reason it is done this way is because it is difficult to tell when the immunities given to the pups through the mother dog's milk wear off and the puppy's own immune system fully kicks in. If you were to find a one-year-old dog on the street and had no idea whether it was ever vaccinated in its entire life, the veterinarian would only give it one series of shots repeated every year because unlike a puppy, a one-year-old dog either has built-up immunities or not.

Knowledgeable dog training schools know how critical it is to take advantage of the sixteen-week window of opportunity that nature has encoded in our puppy's genes. These schools make sure to disinfect the environment and accept puppies that are at least ten weeks old and have had their second series of shots. It's like taking a newborn infant out. Just be reasonable about what you expose them to. Some veterinarians and doggy day cares provide this service as well. They are often called puppy playdates or puppy socializing groups. Check your local resources to find a place that works for you and your puppy. It's a place for puppies to play together safely and learn important lessons such as bite inhibition.

Puppies need to learn how to use their bite pressure while they are still young. We call this bite inhibition, and the best way for them to learn this skill is on each other. Once you remove them from their littermates, they redirect the biting onto you since this is a natural part of growing up as a predator. This is one of the reasons why puppies, not adult dogs, have such needle sharp teeth. As a predator, you must know how to catch, hold, injure, and kill with your teeth. So with needle sharp puppy teeth, it does not take much bite pressure to cause pain to your sibling's ear. When the sibling cries, the biting puppy is learning, while setting new neural pathways, to use and control his bite pressure in the future.

Malamute mix Kayleigh gives Bella and Sparky a warning to play nicely. *Photo by: Julie Aitken.*

As an adult wolf, you must know how to play bite or correct your puppies and other packmates with those same teeth that are used to kill, without causing physical harm, or even send a painful warning without inflicting major injury. A dog's bite must be so accurate because they use their teeth for more than just consuming a meal like we do.

Precise bite pressure insures that the predator is using this tool and weapon to its fullest potential. It's like any hunter. If you don't know how to properly use your equipment, like a bow and arrow, for example, you are at a disadvantage over the hunter who has been practicing this skill since he was a toddler. To the wolf, bite inhibition is a life skill; to our pets, it is as well since a dog that uses his teeth inappropriately gets isolated or euthanized in our society.

This is why it is unreasonable to ask the owner of a German Shepherd dog, Rottweiler, Boxer, Pit Bull, or any other powerful breed to wait until the puppy is five- or six-month-old, large and out of control, to learn what nature intended it to learn its first sixteen weeks of life. I see it all the time. And unfortunately, some of these puppies are so large and powerful by the time they take a class that the owner now has to work twice as hard just to control a puppy that could have been easily influenced prior to reaching this size and strength.

Not to mention, some of these unsocialized puppies have become so chemically unbalanced, just waiting to make contact with another dog that once they finally do, they have no social etiquette and many react aggressively or fearfully since their fight or flight response was left unconditioned by you by not socializing them early. So your dog's nature took your place and set its own neural pathways, and it set the ones that say, "Don't socialize outside your own pack," for you to either recondition or live with.

Having an excited fifty-pound six-month-old pit bull puppy come running up full force to jump on and greet someone with their uninhibited teeth looks more like a threat, then it would have when the same puppy was a cute fifteen-pound ten-week-old baby dog that could have learned not to do that long before he could grow large and become an unbalanced and unmanageable public hazard. Most dogs, puppies, and people don't want to greet a large unruly puppy or dog. This is true for smaller breeds too as I've seen my share of small out of control terrier puppies, for example.

Many owners in this situation give up on training because they are either afraid of their dog using his adult or puppy teeth in a harmful way when making contact with another dog or their unruly behavior triggers an aggressive response from other dogs who just want to keep the threat from coming at them in such an unbalanced way. It is the fight and flight responses, and if a dog or puppy is on a leash and can't *flight* or *avoid,* he might choose *fight* over *submission* if he feels his well-being is going to be threatened since those are the only four choices a predator can make.

Dogs can use their teeth to communicate and to kill or injure, so they must have control of their bite if they are to use them properly. *Photo by: Julie Aitken*

We too are predators. Think about *how you would feel* if an *unbalanced stranger* approached you in an assertive manner. What would your biological (hardware), *nonconditioned response* (classical conditioning) have you make? On the other hand, if you were a trained Martial Arts Master with years of study and *hands-on practice* with similar mock situations (operant conditioning), this talent (software) would give you the edge in controlling the outcome of the situation because you know how the fight, flight, avoidance, and submission mechanism works in both you and your opponent by way of past experience and the neuroassociations that those experiences have produced in the brain.

The Martial Arts Master's ability to anticipate (*conditioned response*) the outcome of a situation and control it is not because he knows how to physically deflect an opponent (operant conditioning); it starts with his ability to control his own brain chemistry by embedding the neural pathway's reactions response through practice and repetition. Once these reactions are preconditioned, they allow us to make efficient use of the brain's ability to help us overcome stressful events according to the challenges we face often. It's a natural survival technique, and aggression is not needed to win in situations where the opponent can be weakened or defeated through mental intimidation or other strategies, first, since aggression draws heavily on the less stable fight and flight biochemical reaction. The martial artist's neural pathways have been preconditioned for him to utilize this adrenaline experience to work for his benefit.

The average person does not encounter unstable strangers often enough to fine-tune and control their own biochemistry. The Martial Arts Master practices mock situations over and over again throughout his career as a master to keep these neural pathways and his skills sharp. People who live in places where danger lurks often either become victims or they sharpen their defenses by being able to control themselves in high stress fight and flight situations. Police officers and our military soldiers are a good example of this since they face unstable people on a daily basis in their jobs, and having this skill means the difference between life and death because that's nature's way.

Many people are too embarrassed to be seen with their unruly dog or puppy because people give them funny looks that suggest they need to train and control their dog. This is where finding the right trainer to help you set new neuroassociations through positive reinforcement methods will help you to overcome this dilemma and move past this situation, creating new neural associations in the brain. The sooner you address these challenges, the sooner you will be enjoying your well-behaved dog in public. Any dog at any age can learn new social skills. The trick is in knowing how to do it properly, without using aggression or intimidation and human will to accomplish the end result.

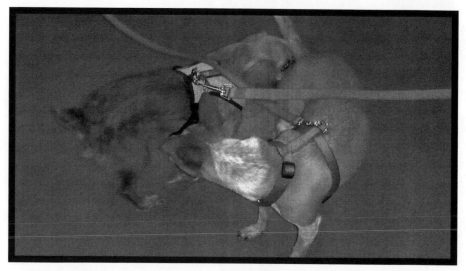

Practicing good leash manners, Crystal and Puppy demonstrate the sniff and be sniffed greeting ritual.

The appropriate way for domestic dogs to meet is the sniff and be sniffed ritual. Sniffing one another's rear ends is like us shaking hands and wanting to know more about each other. Wolves don't do this. They greet mouth-to-mouth. Domestic dogs have their own social rituals and etiquette embedded in their genetics, which need to be practiced and nurtured if they are to socialize respectfully around people and other canines peacefully. Greeting another dog with the mouth-to-mouth wolf approach can elicit a negative response by unsure dogs that might interpret it as a threatening gesture.

GOOD PUPPY ACADEMICS

Unlike the domestic dog's sniff and be sniffed etiquette, wolves greet each other mouth-to-mouth. *John James Henderson/Dreamstime.com*

Dogs are incredibly sensitive to their handler's energy, and most dog owners don't recognize that they are sending signals to their dog that they are uncomfortable during social interactions, thus causing their dog to become in sync with their unsure energy. This message unknowingly tells their dog that its handler thinks something is wrong with the situation, so the dog responds accordingly with unsure energy as well. You must choose a confident trainer who can teach you to relax and take control of the situation and set new patterns and rituals, which are new neuroassociations, that you control not that the dog's primitive nature or the environment controls.

Some dogs need less environmental distractions than others in these situations. Again, seek out a qualified trainer to assist you. Make it fun, and you should be able to recondition your dog. Some dogs are less social than others. This is also seen in us and in the wolf. If you and your dog are the right match, then this does not become a problem because you two are just right for each other; as long as *both of you* are content and happy with this lifestyle, the relationship will be in sync and nonstressful. But if only one of you is content being this way, stress could arise between you.

Unless it is an advanced dog training class or the dogs are aggressive, be sure the trainer allows the friendly dogs and all puppies in a puppy class to socialize and play on leash to show you how it needs to be done correctly and how you should control it, since trainers who do not allow it often don't feel comfortable enough to supervise it properly and end up making the dogs leash aggressive around other dogs; they just wanted to say hello too but were restricted by an unsure handler who was never taught how to introduce their dog appropriately on leash. Leash aggression is simply caused by the handler losing the 0.2 percent of his influence over the 99.8 percent of the dog's primitive nature.

Puppies Spike and Polo enjoy playing nicely on the leash, a skill that helps to eliminate leash aggression later on in their adult lives.

Domestic dogs are somewhat trapped between our human-induced etiquette (what we want) and the wolf's etiquette (what they need). Their wolf genes say to take rank as either an alpha or a submissive. Some pack members even end up as an omega. That's when you are lower than low and are constantly made to submit to your fellow packmates. While the omega wolf is treated poorly, it is still a part of the pack and is protected as a valued member. Omega wolves, however, are sometimes permitted to change ranks, so there is some flexibility in pack dynamics as well. It can change over time depending on the best interests of the pack as a whole.

So find a training school with a trainer that practices good canine etiquette, and school yourself as well with books that are geared toward the sciences that are emerging in the field of canine studies, continuing to fine-tune our knowledge of the awesome world that all of nature is, while sharing our own perspectives with others like I've done here, because Mother Nature knows what she's doing. And we can't say that we know better.

A lot of dog trainers are holding on to outdated training methods and not moving forward in the field of neuroscience and animal behavior. Unfortunately, these "old-school" trainers continue spreading their out-of-date information because they either have no regard for the mental health of the dogs they train, or they just don't know any better. Many choose to intimidate instead of motivate their subjects into learning, but this is a shortcut that makes them more like an opponent than a trusted leader. Some trainers don't care to change their techniques because they still get results by training with harsh methods, and it would mean that they would have to be willing to change their own neuroassociations by reschooling themselves.

Over the last twenty years or so, modern dog trainers and the dog trainer associations and clubs that influence them finally caught up with animal trainers who have been using operant and classical conditioning as their primary methods of training since its earliest beginnings in the labs of Pavlov and Skinner. But there are plenty of old-school dog trainers still using harsh negative reinforcement techniques out there that don't use it. It's a choice *you* have to make. You must decide which school of thought you want to practice and then choose a trainer schooled in these methods and continue to educate yourself. There are many good trainers out there, so find one that suits you and your dog's needs because your dog's state of mental health is as important to him as yours is to you.

What Should My Dog Be Taught First?

House manners should be taught from the first day you bring your new puppy or dog home, even a previously housebroken dog needs to know the rules in its new environment and may even try marking his scent on things to claim his new home. Potty training should be given top priority. Remember the tabula rasa or blank slate theory? That's why it is important for *you* to set and enforce the house rules consistently from the beginning, or your attempts will be in vain. Put the time and effort it takes to succeed in the first few months you have your dog, and you will enjoy living with him for years to come. Expect him to know the rules on his own, you will find yourself constantly complaining about your dog's behavior.

Crate training or some other form of confinement in a laundry room with a baby gate, or a pet playpen in the kitchen, for example, is the best way to have control of your new dog. If you train them to associate these places with their natural tendency to den, the dog will feel secure there. But if you feel bad and see it as a cage or prison for the dog, the dog will fear and get anxious about having to be forced into confinement. There are a lot of ideas and information on how to train this properly. Every dog is different about how they will need to be trained as some will have issues to overcome, such as barking, while others will take to it right away.

It should not take more than one or two weeks to train this behavior if it's introduced correctly and enforced consistently since denning is recognized in their genes. But they must be well-exercised and mentally stimulated enough before they are ever going to be able to rest and enjoy their downtime when you need them to. This downtime needs to be built into their daily patterns and rituals to work effectively.

You can't just store your dog in a room or crate because you have to work or be away. Your dog is a living, intelligent being that will become mentally imbalanced like you would if you were treated that way. Dogs get anxious, depressed, and bored like us, and they can suffer the same or even worse mental stress than we do since they have no right to complain. Unless a law is broken, there is no one to protect them from their owner's actions if they do.

Bringing a new dog or puppy home should be seen as a serious commitment. Setting the basic foundation the first year that you have your dog and consistently practicing each behavior until the dog can do it reliably anywhere you ask will help you to create a relationship that you will enjoy for years to come. It takes time, effort, patience, and dedication to train a dog that is reliable. Some dogs learn quicker than others, but they all need the same consistency, motivation, and encouragement to be the best they can be.

So as you can see, you have a lot to teach. But these things are not so difficult if you know how to train the brain. Obedience training and socialization around as many people, pets, sights, sounds, and smells as possible is critical for any dog but especially puppies. Use treats and keep it fun and interesting for the dog, so he will eventually want to repeat those embedded behaviors later without treats. Basic obedience such as walking on a loose leash, sit, down, stay, release, here, watch me, come, give, drop it, leave it, out and off are a great place to start.

If your puppy is at least ten weeks old, is healthy, and has had its second series of shots, then joining a group puppy obedience training class to train and socialize your puppy in, which uses positive reinforcement, is a great avenue to start out training the brain on how to work with distractions. Socializing with many different breeds of dogs and puppies safely is also a must. Be sure to only socialize around safe animals. Always make training and socializing fun and rewarding, and your dog should become a well-balanced adult. Negative experiences or challenges can set you back but should always be seen as opportunities to help you and your dog grow.

Many dogs and puppies get uncomfortable when greeting strangers, so socializing needs to be done in a positive way. You cannot force a dog or puppy into it. You must give it some time to assess the situation and become comfortable enough to learn from the experience. *Keep in mind how the brain game works.* If you do things that cause a puppy or dog discomfort when training it to like people, the dog will just learn to practice avoidance behavior or become more and more anxious about meeting people, causing a negative biochemical response. You must make these encounters pleasant for the dog. *This will allow you to influence and set the neural pathways as a pleasant biochemical response* instead of the high adrenaline fight or flight or avoidance response.

There are many situations where dogs get stressed when people hover over them or reach out and pet them. After a while, some dogs might start seeing this pattern as an invasion of space or as a threat. These are natural responses to the dog. In order to change the response, you must make these events more positive in the dog's mind. The more bad experiences the dog has while greeting people, the less likely it is to overcome it. If your dog is not people or food aggressive, you can try using real chicken, or other high-value food, to override the dog's emotions with scent. Overwhelming the nose will usually redirect the dog's attention and cause *the food-motivated dog* to try and figure out what it needs to do to gain access to the reward. As long as you're sure the dog will not bite anyone, let people know your dog is getting used to socializing, and they can help by giving it a treat. Petting is not necessary at first if your dog is hand shy. If your dog is very scared, start by socializing it at home so not to overwhelm it in a public setting.

If you fail to change the behavior right away, the pattern will continue to drive the dog's reaction and probably escalate it over time. In other words, if the dog's undesired reaction was not properly addressed and eliminated when it first began, the dog's neural pathways will become conditioned to react that way over and over again. To recondition the brain's neural pathways, you must make the experience pleasant for the dog rather than make it unpleasant since greeting people needs to be a good experience.

Potty Training

Potty training requires patience and strategy on your part. It is a twenty-four-hour-a-day, seven-day-a-week job. *Efficiently trained* (full time), a puppy or dog can be potty-trained in as little as two weeks. *Trained inefficiently* (part time), it can take months and in many cases will become difficult to break. The truth is that it is *you who will decide* how long it takes to potty-train your new dog or puppy, so you should have a strategy in place before bringing your new pet into your home. Buy a potty-training book, video, or go online and find information there.

There are many ways to potty-train. Find what works well for your dog and your lifestyle. Set and enforce the pattern from day one onto his *blank slate.* Or your dog will set his own patterns and write his own slate. Practice umbilical cord bonding. This is done by keeping the puppy or dog attached to you with the leash for the first two weeks; you have your dog whenever it's in the house, and you can't closely supervise it. That way it can't wander off to potty since it is always near you and directed by you whenever it's awake. Being consistent is the key to teaching a new behavior in the shortest amount of time.

Take your new puppy out every hour at first, just to get a solid pattern set, but don't give them more than five minutes to go potty. Have them on a four-to-six-foot leash and just stand in one spot. Don't walk around following the dog or puppy, but do allow it to walk wherever it wants and sniff the environment within the length of the leash. If he pulls at the end, just don't move, and he will eventually give up, or call him closer to you and praise him for staying near you while you remind him again to go potty.

They need to understand it's not time to play and explore, it's time to eliminate. Have a word or phrase associated with eliminating. I say better hurry; some people say go potty. It doesn't matter what you say as long as the puppy or dog understands what it means. This is how service dogs are taught to eliminate on command. Once the puppy eliminates, you can take it off the leash and celebrate the victory with a treat and play or exploring the yard. If it does not eliminate within five minutes, go back inside. After ten or fifteen minutes, try again since the puppy is attached to you with the leash; if he eliminates in the house, you will be able to catch him in the act and calmly but quickly stop him and redirect him to the appropriate place.

Interrupting the neuroassociation by catching the brain right when it's thinking of doing it, or as it's engaged, is a powerful way to short circuit, so to speak, the neural pathway so it's recalled later the same interrupted way if the dog thinks of doing that again. But you must not get mad or convey panic when you catch the dog eliminating. We do not want it to become fearful. Just use a low monotone and say something like, "Ah, ah nope! Let's potty outside," then take the dog out or to the potty pad and hope he continues to eliminate there. If he does, be sure to celebrate with higher pitch praise and a treat or reward them with play. If he doesn't, try walking him around outside (don't let him walk you) for five minutes. They will often eliminate then and give you an opportunity to mark the behavior as it happens. It's about not letting the puppy set his own pattern. And it is you who controls that.

Use only one door as the exit at first to go potty. This should set a pattern that will enable the dog to learn quickly where he or she should go to alert you when it needs to go outside. Do not free feed your puppy. Offer food two or three times a day as directed by the dog food feeding instructions or your veterinarian, and remove it after fifteen minutes if the dog does not eat it all. This will help regulate the frequency of elimination, allowing you to better predict when your dog might need to go. Always use positive reinforcement methods anytime you train your dog or puppy. Providing your dog is healthy, all dogs can be potty-trained. It is not about breed, age, or smarts on the dog's part. It's about how effective you are in showing a dog where you expect it to eliminate as it only knows what you allow it to learn and continue repeating.

CHAPTER 3

Good Puppy Academics Program

USING THE FOLLOWING *Good Puppy Academics* progress reports and your knowledge about the brain game, patterns and rituals and what's in your dog, you can train the basic skills your pet needs to be a lifelong canine good citizen at home and in public. Puppies and dogs love to learn new things. It is embedded in them to be curious and to problem-solve if given the opportunity to prove themselves through experience.

With a smile on his face, five-year-old American Bulldog Kong graduates from beginner's obedience class, proving that you can teach an old unwanted rescue dog new tricks.

Students depend on their mentors for success. If your canine student isn't cooperating, change your approach and find another more effective way to influence it. Communication is the key to being an effective mentor. Understanding your student's body language and behaviors is feedback which enables you to effectively interact with your subject. You began to *see and feel the impact of your efforts* as you guide your canine student to reach its fullest potential. Remember, motivation not intimidation is the key to success.

Use positive reinforcement. It is the most effective way to teach. Emphasis and reward is focused on positive behaviors, while undesired behaviors are corrected, redirected, or ignored. Consistent leadership, praise, and appreciation are the motivation for learning, while *the dog chooses* a rewarding consequence over an unrewarding one. Have fun and be creative, and both of you will enjoy the process as you learn together nature's way.

Good Puppy Academics

Grade: C   *Assigned to all new "students."*

I = Introduced   Used to identify the first time a new skill is introduced.

L = Learning   Used when your dog is showing signs of understanding your direction.

Grade: B   *Assigned to advancing students.*

K = Knows   Used to show that dog knows the skill and will perform it most of the time. May still be using treats.

R = Refining   Used while training dog to generalize skill to perform whenever and wherever it is *asked* to, with distraction, without treats, and by voice command, in order to reach the next grade level: *A* = exceptional student.

C = Average Student

This grade is assigned to any dog learning a new skill. Starting with an average dog or puppy, it is the goal of the mentor to teach new skills and then bring the dog to the next grade level.

B = Above Average Student

This grade is assigned when a new skill has been learned. The dog will perform most of the time and is being weaned from the treats.

A = Exceptional Student

This grade is assigned when a learned skill has been generalized by *the dog*, who will perform it anywhere and at any time when asked to by mentor without treats, *with* some behaviors being automatic.

Good Puppy Academics

Report Card

Assessment of Individual Growth

Start Date: _____ / _____ / _____

Insert your dog's picture here

Dog's Name: _____ Age: _____

Dog's Birthday: _____

Using Nature's Way to Raise Your Dog's GPA

List of Skills

Yes!	Marks the behavior. The millisecond of success! *Must* always be followed by a treat.
Nope	Marks an undesired behavior. Used to fine-tune the dog's skills. Simply means "that's not what I asked," followed by redirection and praise. Keeps you from repeating the command over and over. Nope; sounds very different than "No!" which is what you say when the dog is caught doing something wrong like getting into in the kitchen garbage or stealing food off your dinner plate, for example. *That's a correction.*
Good job	Lets your dog know you are pleased with its behavior.
Here	Dog should come to the place designated by a finger-point. Use when dog is on leash or off leash.
That's it	Encourages and guides dog. Used to let him know he is on the right track. Also used as motivation.
Thank you	Shows appreciation for the dog's willingness to work.
Better hurry	Tells dog that now is the time and place to toilet.
Let's go	Dog walks with a loose leash, with sniffing allowed.
Quiet	Dog is to stop growling, whining, or barking.
Sit	Dog should put its bottom on ground and be in a sitting position.
Come	Calls your dog to you. Dog should come running. Use only when dog is off leash.
Down	Dog should lower its entire body to the ground.
Dress	Dog should slip its head through the opening of its collar, harness, cape, or backpack.

- Training tip: Communication is the key to being an effective mentor. If you understand your dog's body language and behaviors, they become feedback which enables you to effectively interact with your dog.

Skill	/ Grade/	WK 1/	WK 2/	WK 3/	WK 4 /	Grade / Date
Dog's name	C					
Yes!	C					
Nope!	C					
Good job	C					
Here	C					
That's it	C					
Thank you	C					
Better hurry	C					
Let's go	C					
Quiet	C					
Sit	C					
Come	C					
Down	C					
Dress	C					

Trainer's notes: _____

_____

_____

_____

_____

Good Puppy Academics

Report Card

Assessment of Individual Growth

Start Date: _____/_____/_____

```
┌─────────────────────────────────────┐
│                                       │
│                                       │
│     Insert your dog's picture here    │
│                                       │
│                                       │
│                                       │
└─────────────────────────────────────┘
```

Dog's Name: _____ Age: _____

Dog's Birthday: _____

Using Nature's Way to Raise Your Dog's GPA

List of Skills

Speak	Dog barks on your command.
Up	Tells dog to place its front paws up onto a person, counter, or other object.
Off	Instructs dog to remove its front paws from a counter or to remove itself from an object.
Fix	Dog should untangle its leash from around an object or its own legs.
Shake	Dog lifts left or right paw from a standing or sitting position.
Roll	Instructs dog to lie down and expose its belly or can be used to have dog roll completely over.
Jump on	Dog is to leap onto a designated object or onto your lap.
Go in	Tells dog to lie down under something out of the way.
Out	Sends dog out of a room or area.
Settle	Dog is to settle down, relax, and behave.
Wait	Instructs dog not to cross a threshold until given permission. Also can be used to say, "Hold on a minute." Wait is not the same as stay.
Turn	Instructs dog to turn around and face the opposite direction. Start with a full circle.

- *Feel the impact of your efforts.* As a mentor, you are guiding your student to reach their fullest potential. Motivation is the key to success.

Skill	/ Grade/	WK 1/	WK 2/	WK 3/	WK 4/	Grade / Date
Speak	C					
Up	C					
Off	C					
Fix	C					
Shake	C					
Roll	C					
Jump on	C					
Go in	C					
Out	C					
Settle	C					
Wait	C					
Turn	C					

Trainer's notes: _____

_____

_____

_____

_____

Good Puppy Academics

Level Three

Report Card

Assessment of Individual Growth

Start Date: _____/_____/_____

Insert your dog's picture here

Dog's Name: _____ Age: _____

Dog's Birthday: _____

Using Nature's Way to Raise Your Dog's GPA

List of Skills

Leave it	Instructs the dog not to touch an item or to ignore whatever it has taken an interest in.
Stay	Instructs dog not to move from its position or place.
Release	Instructs dog that it can break its stay and is free to go.
Heel	Dog must position itself on your left side facing forward. Should walk at your pace with a loose leash. No sniffing allowed. Right side acceptable if you wish.
Closer	Tells dog to move nearer to you or an object. Can also be used when they need to loosen a tight leash.
Get it	Directs dog to retrieve an item.
Give	Instructs dog to give you retrieved item, placing it in your hand.
Tug	Tells dog to tug on a rope. Can also be used to have them open a door or cupboard.
Push	Instructs dog to push a door or cupboard shut with its paw(s).
Drop it	Instructs dog to release whatever he has in his mouth without your hand being on the object.
Bed	Instructs dog to go into its crate or onto its bed.

- *It's always the trainer never the dog.* Students depend on their mentors for success. If your student isn't cooperating, change your approach.

Skill	/ Grade	/ WK 1	/ WK 2	/ WK 3	/ WK 4	/ Grade	/ Date
Leave it	C						
Stay	C						
Release	C						
Heel	C						
Closer	C						
Get it	C						
Give	C						
Tug	C						
Push	C						
Drop it	C						
Bed	C						

Trainer's notes: _____

_____

_____

_____

_____

Good Puppy Academics

Report Card

Assessment of Individual Growth

Start Date: _____/_____/_____

$$\boxed{\text{Insert your dog's picture here}}$$

Dog's Name: _____ Age: _____

Dog's Birthday: _____

Using Nature's Way to Raise Your Dog's GPA

- *Positive reinforcement.* The best way to teach. Emphasis and reward is focused on positive behaviors, while undesired behaviors are redirected or ignored. Praise and appreciation is the key.

List of Skills

_____

_____

_____

_____

_____

_____

_____

_____

_____

- *Trigger thinking.* Teach your student how to think. Let them be part of the problem-solving effort, asking the dog to focus on the result, the goal.

Skill	/ Grade/	WK 1/	WK 2/	WK 3/	WK 4/	Grade /	Date

Trainer's notes: _____

_____

_____

_____

_____

Being a Responsible k9 Guardian

Congratulation! By choosing to train and learn more about your dog, you are now a more knowledgeable and responsible canine guardian. You and your pet will appreciate this balanced way of life, and you will both be happy to spend your days living together. Now you can reap the benefits of your efforts by taking your dog anywhere you can without the stress of having nature or "the wild within" come out and challenge you or others. By knowing your dog's patterns in public, you become a better handler as you showcase your dog's social talent. If your dog trusts you, then you can do just about anything, providing the dog is capable of what you are requiring of it.

Knowing how to read a dog's state of mind through its body language is also critical if you are to communicate in their language. *You already communicate with them* through scent molecules called pheromones that you can't control. And your body language backs that up. Remember, domestic dogs have been studying humans for about fifteen thousand years, so you better catch up and learn about them what they already know about you. Here is where understanding the fight, flight, submission, and avoidance responses in your own dog becomes critical since these are predators only choices in life.

For our domestic dogs, the ideal state is that of submission since fight, flight, and avoidance are considered antisocial and dangerous in our society. Excitement is expected in some working dogs, such as police, hunting, tracking, search, and rescue dogs, but in our pets, we often expect and prefer a calmer state of mind and energy *to keep us comfortable*. If you don't want a dog or puppy with excited energy, then don't choose the Labrador retriever, terrier, or mix breed that is all over you and wants to go, go, and go.

These dogs need a lot of exercise and mental stimulation to be well-balanced pets; instead, choose a more submissive, relaxed energy within that breed that's in your range of choices. For example, when choosing a Labrador retriever for hunting, you must have a dog that can calmly, yet eagerly, lay in wait for the hunter to instruct it to go and get the targeted prey. The retriever then gets excited and runs or swims to retrieve the prize but delivers it to the hunter in a calm, controlled, and respectful manner. This is true of a good hunting dog.

Labrador and Golden retrievers are great swimmers and love to run and play off leash. They require a lot of exercise.

But if you are choosing a Labrador retriever to look for narcotics, you would choose the most high energy, playful, toy-driven, people-loving, curious, and active lab you could find, one whose drive engages him in an almost unhealthy, obsessive way. Not a good energy to have if you are expected to exhibit the patience of a good hunter or are asked to live in an apartment or yard all day. But if you get to channel this obsessive energy looking for the smell of narcotics, which represents a much anticipated reward like playing with your favorite ball, you are considered a valued member of society. If you are a pet and are not given an outlet to expend this mental and physical energy, you become a problem dog.

A German Shepherd police dog, barking uncontrollably in the back of a police car or lunging at the end of a leash trying to get to a suspect, appears aggressive, untrained, and out of control. These dogs are permitted to display behaviors that are intimidating in an attempt to give the suspect a choice to either surrender peacefully, so no one gets hurt, or sufferer the consequence of having the police dog subdue him with its teeth.

What you see in the police dog is not aggression; it's a warning, and it's actually part of the dog's training. The officer's preference is to not have to release his dog as there is always a chance the person or dog could be injured, once the dog's fight response kicks in and aggression surfaces *as a result of the adrenaline rush experienced to protect him* during this dangerous high stress encounter. Under the control of an inexperienced, irresponsible handler, these dogs would be a seriously dangerous threat.

A police dog cannot pose a threat to the general public. Police dogs are not taught to attack the suspect either; it's never about aggression; that's a natural response once the pursuit begins; they are trained to pursue, hold, and subdue the suspect (like some hunting dogs do), so the handler can gain control of the situation before calling off his dog. Police dogs are under the full control of their handlers; otherwise, they would be dangerous to us and the handler.

Wolves do this as well when they hunt. During the *pursuit,* the first wolf that makes contact with large prey tries to *hold and subdue* the animal while the others rush in, like teamwork, to help and kill it. For the police dog and the officer, the same teamwork ends without the kill or severe injury. That's the point of using the police dog. It's safer for everyone. The suspect can choose fight, flight, avoidance, or submission, but the dog will always win as long as the suspect does not manage to get away or kill the dog because that's nature's way, and we incorporate it in the police k9 team for the good of society.

These same behaviors would be undesired in a pet and could lead to this same wonderful dog, that we admire and appreciate for its public service, to be euthanized. If this German Shepherd dog was your pet and you permitted it to display these behaviors, he would be dangerous and you would be a very irresponsible k9 guardian. Police dogs are not only well-trained, but their skills must be managed by the police officer who handles them on a daily basis to maintain the standards needed to keep the dog's work ethics stable and reliable.

I can't tell you how many times I've heard German Shepherd dog owners say they got the dog so they could practice Schutzhund or protection training with it. While Schutzhund training has become a popular sport, it was originally created by the Germans in the 1900s as a test to see which German Shepherd dogs could handle the stress and demands of being a police dog. Traits such as courage and drive with the will to work and protect their handler along with intelligence, agility, endurance, and strength were tested, and only the dogs that could get through the rigorous training successfully were chosen for various types of police work like search and rescue, scent detection, guarding, and attack work.

The German Shepherd dog was originally bred to be a flock herder and guardian, so not every German Shepherd dog makes a good police dog. Our police and military dogs are all Schutzhund trained to insure the right dog is doing this work as not every dog tested and trained pass the requirements needed for this intense and important job. An aggressive, overdominate dog might be eliminated by this form of testing as a police dog but might be a good candidate as a war dog, where the rules are different. Since making the kill is not necessarily off-limits, while the dogs that work as police k9s among us in society must not kill.

So, is there a place in society to be a pet for the wild high energy Labrador retriever who needs a home or the unsocialized German Shepherd dog who is dominant or aggressive? Absolutely! But these dogs must be in the right hands to succeed since they will not be working in the jobs they were "hardwired" to do when we decided to create them *for our benefit*. So the Labrador retriever that can't stop moving around needs a good cardio workout at least five or six days a week with some mental stimulation and a daily dose of activities such as hiking, swimming, ball chasing, running beside a bicycle, or with someone on skates, and playing and socializing with other dogs outside of their own home pack at a dog park or doggy day care center, in addition to activities such as agility. Obedience training is important and must be a priority as well.

Labrador retrievers Lulu and Tessa enjoy practicing their splash dog skills while playing in their own yard.

Splash dogs is a water sport these labs adore. Look into these resources. If you are not active and willing to do these types of activities, then don't get a high energy Labrador. The same holds true for the German Shepherd dog. You must find a suitable way to channel its physical and mental energy for it to succeed at being a great pet. If you do choose Schutzhund training, *you must* be dedicated in maintaining the dog's skills like the police officer does, by joining Schutzhund groups and competing in trials to uphold the standards needed to retain the dog's work ethics, stability, and reliability. Just like the Martial Arts Master, if you don't keep those neural pathways working every day, nature will take over and start resetting what you fail to keep conditioned. Once trained, you are just keeping the weeds from overtaking the pathways you set. If you don't, the dog will be a danger to you, himself, and others.

There are all kinds of different temperaments within every dog breed whether mixed or purebred. *Channeling their energy means capitalizing on the innate abilities you wish to accentuate* because that's what's in your dog. Remember?

Good Puppy Etiquette

So we know dogs and wolves have their own social etiquette as do we. If a dog is to live successfully in both these worlds, *we* must know how to engage them properly in both human and canine social styles. By understanding the conversations dogs have with each other and what our social etiquette requires of them, we can create the situations we want rather than waiting for situations to occur, so we can address them then. Social interactions become either patterns you set or the dog sets. When you set them, the dog has the opportunity to learn and practice good associations that should eventually become *automatic behaviors* that you like.

When dogs meet for the first time, they should take an interest in each other by sniffing the air to try and catch the scent of the other dog. This is nature's way of allowing animals to get a sense of one another without physical contact first. Air scenting is how predators and the animals they prey upon keep themselves safe. At the same time, body language is being spoken as they communicate silently. Knowing what their conversation is *before* they make physical contact is the key to being *a great* dog handler. Believe it or not, some of their body language and vocal tones are *exactly* like ours; they share the same meaning and what's obvious to us in human body language and vocal tones can also become obvious in dog form to the trained eye. This is because we are all animals, and *Mother Nature always keeps it simple*. In the wild, if it takes you a long period of time to figure out the intentions of another animal, you're in big trouble and probably won't live very long.

For example, in human terms, low vocal tones usually convey a more serious message than a high-pitch sound that attracts us and conveys a happy, sometimes excited, pleasant message. The inflection of the sound helps to fine-tune what the intensity of the message being sent is as does the volume. A dog's growl is our equivalent to sending a vocal message that conveys a warning in hopes to detour or defuse a situation so that we won't have to take the next step, which could turn into a physical confrontation. It's a way of standing your ground without hostility, in hopes that your opponent will walk away. It can also mean that the predator is simply annoyed or frustrated and wants to disengage from a situation, like our equivalent of grumbling.

High-pitched tones seem to attract our attention in a different way than low tones. That's nature's hardwiring and it serves us well. So using these happy, attractive tones on your dog helps to keep their attention and sets "feel-good" endorphin-induced neural pathways that encourage the predator to cooperate. Wolf pups instinctually use these tones which triggers the adults to nurture and care for them. Monotones can work too, depending on the situation and reaction it gets from your dog. When high, mono, and low tones are used correctly, they serve as an audio way of controlling and setting your dog's neural pathways instead of in a hands-on way. It's not the words you use but how you say them that tell the dog what you mean because dogs don't understand human language as we know it.

Eyes, ears, nose, and mouth are the predator's tools, and it serves us well to know how they use them. Let's take a closer look at the predator's natural abilities when using these instruments. The predator only uses his nose to find food or a mate, smell danger, or identify things that he cannot see. This is like a tracking dog. It is a neutral state of mind that is not concerned with fight, flight, submission, or avoidance. It's just interested in the environment and what its chemical signals have to say. But once it finds a chemical trail that attracts its attention, the predator's state of mind changes to wanting to get a visual conformation of where the trail ends. Once visual contact is made, the predator's eyes take over to assess the situation. This is when either fight, flight, avoidance, submission, or a predatory state of mind kicks in.

If the predator, like a wolf, sees an easy target, like a juvenile deer that has left its mother's side, he will automatically start going through a predictable sequence of behaviors. These patterns are hardwired in their brains and perfected from infancy through adulthood during play and by their families "hands-on" teachings. After making visual contact with its prey, the predator will go into a stalking mode, trying to remain undetected to get close enough to succeed at making physical contact with its target, by using the least amount of energy and effort to catch it; since once it is caught, the fight or flight response will kick in, and it will take a lot of energy and skill to win the battle over life and death. Remember, in the natural world, the rule for all predators is *no skill no kill.*

Once the predator is as close as he can get without being detected by the target, he will charge and try to subdue it as soon as possible before it can smell, hear, or see him coming and run for its life. If the predator is successful, he will be able to take down and kill this prey quickly and efficiently with the least amount of danger or effort. This is the ideal situation since having to run down and herd your prey takes a lot more calories and skill to win, and the animal might even hurt you to survive the attack. The stakes and risks are a lot higher once your opponent gets an edge on you. Human hunters practice these same strategies because it's hardwired in us as well.

A daring move for any animal. This wolf doesn't stand a chance if this mother bear manages to catch him. So his *flight* chemical reaction kicks in to give him a chance at survival. *Hakoar/Dreamstime.com*

With her bear cubs looking on, this wolf's adrenaline reaction saves it from sure disaster as the mother bear's adrenaline pumps her up with the *fight* chemical reaction. *Hakoar/Dreamstime.com*

But what if a hungry predator, like a wolf, encounters a bear cub at the end of the scent trail that has strayed too far from its mother's side? Unlike the deer parent who is not a predator and cannot protect her young as efficiently as another predator can, the bear cub's mother poses a serious risk to anyone who wants to eat her baby. So the hungry wolf faced with this choice would choose flight or avoidance if its mother was too near and capitalize more on hunting the animals who don't want to eat them in return. This analogy illustrates that there are always choices to make in which individual situations call for different individual problem-solving strategies depending on what's good for you.

We can see these same hunting behaviors clearly in the Border Collie, whose stalking and herding strategies are closest to the wolf compared to any other domestic dog breed. We capitalized on this part of the hunt when we genetically selected the genes that create the Border Collie as we know it today, but we took the kill out of their bite in that 0.2 percent of the wolf's genes that we altered to domesticate and *neotenize* them. Border Collies are never allowed to move the sheep with aggression. They can move them with some intimidation but must not inflict injury or cause panic while doing it. If you see them working, they keep their tails low instead of riding high in the air or curved over their back, and there is no need for the nose to engage as the targets are always visual. You can see and feel the intensity in their stare as the predator within strategically stalks and moves the prey.

Domestic sheep still carry a strong genetic flight reaction when threatened by a predator, so the Border Collie must not scare them into scattering. *Clearviewstock/Dreamstime.com*

Tail carriage gives us insight into what *state of mind* the Border Collie is in while moving the sheep. A calm demeanor means that the quick assertive energy the Border Collie is giving out does not send the sheep into a frantic fight or flight situation like it would if the Border Collie's intent was to capture the sheep. Instead, the sheep remain in more of a submission and avoidance state of mind since the Border Collie doesn't pose a real threat. A tail in the air signifies that the dog's intent has now shifted to a more assertive and dominant energy that lets the other animal know it is confident, dominant, and able to stand up for itself and likes to be noticed as such. This kind of energy is not necessary for moving herds of domestic sheep.

Cattle dogs must be more assertive and careful as the animals they move are larger and dangerous. Resembling the herds wolves pursue, but these dogs don't catch and kill.
Belinda Pretorius | Dreamstime.com

Cattle dogs work differently since they are moving larger more dangerous and dominant animals. Moving cattle requires a different strategy and mind-set to control them. But you still must inhibit your bite and not spook them, severely injure, or kill them either. In fact, there are laws that protect livestock from attacks by domestic dogs. A rancher has the right to shoot and kill any dog that threatens the well-being of their animals. A lot of horses, llamas, and other large farm animals die every year as a result of domestic dog attacks, and it is a very serious offence. For one thing, aggression or killing is not necessarily a dog's motivation for going after another animal. Just the excitement of chasing something that's trying to avoid you can trigger some dog's hardwired need to pursue, grab, and bite to control the movement, much like what drives the police dog.

This behavior is seen when a dog chases a ball, for example. He gets to chase it, catch it, and bite it. But there is no law protecting balls, so once a dog transfers this behavior onto a four-legged furry target, the stakes are high. Sadly, some children and adults have suffered the same fate by untrained, unsocialized, and dangerous dogs and some by dogs whose intent was driven by instinct, and aggression surfaced as a result of high adrenaline chemicals flooding the predator's system to prepare and protect him from a counterattack by the animal in flight trying to escape capture. It's quick, automatic, and dangerous when not noticed and addressed before something like that happens. These dogs can and must be taught *impulse control.* Something the Border Collie and cattle dog have mastered.

Animals that live in herds naturally move together as a group. It is the wolf who capitalized on their patterns in the wild and invented the herding dog, not us. The wolf figured out a long time ago how their prey's fight, flight, avoidance, or submission response could work for them instead of against them during the hunt and how they must control their own impulsive actions so their adrenaline does not work against them during these split-second life-or-death moments that a wolf encounters often throughout its lifetime.

GOOD PUPPY ACADEMICS

Our domestic dogs are not that savvy because they are not supposed to concern themselves with life-and-death situations everyday like the wolf or Martial Arts Master does. So we must set those pathways our way and keep them active through practice to avoid unpredictable, impulsive behaviors to get the best of our dogs.

So how do you want your dog's etiquette to be at home and in public places? The most important things to consider are your families, the publics, and your dog's safety. Think about what manners you expect in public from your friends and family members and expect the same from your dog. Be consistent with addressing behaviors that you don't like, so they can't become patterns that set in and get harder to break. Remember, if you are complaining about your dog's behavior, that means it's a pattern you need to change or live with. The choice falls on you, not the dog.

The American Kennel Club offers the Canine Good Citizen's test for all dogs regardless of the mix or breed, which serves as a good guideline that you can incorporate in your daily training routine to help and keep you focused on the importance of good canine and handler practices. When you and your dog are ready, take the test. If your dog is not the right temperament to pass this test, just make sure you still make him practice good etiquette whenever you are at home or out in public. Even antisocial dogs can be taught to have manners. But you must set them up to succeed and keep them from situations where they are sure to fail. This is where private or group obedience training is important. You and your dog or puppy will learn to interact as a team rather than as individuals, who each have a different social agenda when out together in public.

Enjoying Your Dog in Public Places

Everyone enjoys and admires a well-behaved dog. If you have done your homework, there is no reason your dog shouldn't accompany you in public wherever pets are permitted to go or to gatherings with friends and vacation with family. Dogs that are social enjoy these interactions as much as we do and deserve to be rewarded by being allowed to participate. If your dog is not social and would not be comfortable with these activities, then find other times to incorporate the dog into your life, like taking it for a car ride, somewhere for a walk, or a picnic. My dog and I do a lot of things together that doesn't require socializing with others, and sometimes, we do depending on the activity.

Canine Good Citizen Russo, is always included in family activities as they enjoy sharing their adventures together.

Enjoying your pet is the reason you have it. Remember, your pet should be a stress reducer not a stress producer. If you are not enjoying your life with a dog, then the dog is not enjoying

GOOD PUPPY ACADEMICS

its life with your either. But a lot of people don't enjoy their dog or puppy simply because they don't know how. That is why joining *the right* training class is important. You would be surprised at how much you'll appreciate being educated when you see the results of your efforts manifest in your dog. What you thought would be difficult to train is actually doable once you have hands-on experience and understanding of how the power of your own actions can influence your pet.

Training builds up the confidence and trust needed for the human and canine partnership to flourish and expand as both canine and human neural pathways get set together. All dogs and their handlers need training, and all dogs and their handlers benefit from it regardless of age, past experiences, or temperament. The science of *neuroplasticity* has proven that the brain is flexible and changes throughout our life. We can influence some of these changes ourselves if only we know how.

Having control of your dog in social situations must be taught. Enjoying your dog's public etiquette will encourage you to show off his talents that you both worked hard to achieve. Training is teamwork. Don't look at your relationship as a "boss and worker" team. Look at it more as a "coach and athlete" partnership. A boss and a coach are not the same. A boss dictates what his subjects must do, while a coach drives and motivates his subjects to achieve success one step at a time. A boss needs to keep order in his subjects, and a coach needs to keep balance in his. Both are instructors and supervisors, but one is a leader with a strict agenda that leads with authority and the other leads with creativity based on his subject's individual need. A coach mentors, while a boss is more ridged about how things must be done. Upholding standards according to a specific set of rules is something coaches and bosses do, but their jobs are done much different.

In the wolf pack, the adults are bossed and the pups are mentored. That's why it is critical for you to mentor your canine student instead of boss him around. Keep tapping into the 0.2 percent of the genes we manipulated in our pets, and stay away from the 99.8 percent of their wild side, and you will succeed at training the brain to remain in a more cooperative and submissive state of mind. Socializing must be positive and rewarding for anyone to enjoy it.

So coach your subject, then showcase his talents, and you will experience positive feedback as your audience appreciates your routine and your team discipline. Besides, no one likes to see an out of control human trying to control their out of control dog. We have to learn to address our dogs in a calm and assertive manner not in an angry, frustrated, or forceful one. Remember, your dog is a reflection of you. If you want calm, get calm first, then try convincing your dog to match your energy. Don't match theirs. Fighting resistance with resistance never works and causes more stress in the situation.

CHAPTER 4

Service dog Gizmo enjoys being a copilot in more than one way as he mitigates and navigates for his partner.

Assistance Dogs
(What Is an Assistance Dog?)

THE TERM *ASSISTANCE dog* is used to describe a dog that mitigates a person's disability by performing one or more physical tasks to assist their partner. Guide dogs, hearing dogs, mobility service dogs, medical alert service dogs, and psychiatric service dogs are all assistance dogs. Therapy dogs and pets are not recognized under the law as assistance dogs. They are companion dogs because they do not perform a *physical task* to mitigate a person's disability. They just keep you company and make you feel good.

Liesl, a yellow lab, has learned to retrieve a water bottle and loves performing the task as Labrador retrievers were genetically created for this purpose.

Liesl was taught to drop the bottle through positive reinforcement methods instead of using negative reinforcement like the ear pinch.

There is a huge gray area about the difference between a mobility service dog and a psychiatric service dog. The truth is there is no difference between the two. Both are considered service dogs as long as they perform *at least one physical task* for their partner. So the only difference between a mobility service dog and a psychiatric service dog is the task(s) they perform to mitigate a person's disability whether mental or physical. All service dogs should be trained to pass the American Kennel Club's Canine Good Citizen's test as well as the Assistance Dogs International standard test for public access to be a stable and reliable working dog in all public places.

Assistance dogs are different than pets as the work they are asked to do and the tasks they are required to execute are beyond what the average pet needs to know. Not many dogs can handle the rigors of what we ask an assistance dog to do. All assistance dogs should have automatic behaviors when it comes to etiquette. Once fully trained, an assistance dog should not have to be reminded everyday how to behave when working. It should be preconditioned to not be obstructive in public situations, follow its partner automatically on a loose leash, and ignore the environmental distractions that bombard it, as well as be available and willing to work whenever a helping hand is needed.

Training a reliable service dog is hard work and usually takes one to two years of consistent exposure and fine-tuning in order for the dog to become the safe and reliable helpmate it needs to be. Other than being protected by humane animal laws, assistance dogs have no rights. It is the human they serve who has the right to utilize a dog to mitigate their disability.

In the eyes of the federal law, the assistance dog is nothing more than a medical aid, no different than a cane or a wheelchair. It is used like medical equipment. So when any business denies an assistance dog user access to their establishment with their dog, they are, in fact, denying the disabled individual access due to their disability, not because they have a dog. It's like telling a blind person to leave his eyeglasses in the car or an amputee to leave his prosthetic device outside if they want to enjoy public access rights in their business.

There are people who take their pet dogs with them everywhere and say they are assistance dogs when, in fact, they have not been trained as such. Some people rationalize that their pet is an assistance dog because either they or their pet get anxious when apart. This is not a legitimate reason to take a dog where pets are not permitted. This is something they and their dog must overcome. It's not a disability; it's an emotional imbalance, and it's not healthy for either one of them. Help should be sought out for this type of problem if it is affecting a person's lifestyle in a way that makes them break the laws that assistance dog users protect, respect, and count on in order to have *the privilege* of working their well-trained dogs in public.

If people believe pet dogs should be allowed everywhere in public, then they need to do what Bonnie Bergin and the guide dog organization founders and users did and have the laws changed instead of riding on the coattails of someone else's hard work to take advantage of the situation. It may not seem like a big deal, but it is to someone who counts on the laws to protect their right to use an assistance dog.

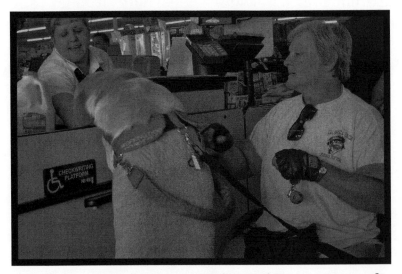

Working together as a team, Elaine and Pogo are a perfect match. Service dogs perform vital tasks for their partners.

It was not easy for Bonnie Bergin to convince lawmakers that a service dog would not pose a public hazard when working. These lawmakers would see a quadriplegic with a large dog, and convincing them that an immobile person could have control and the dog would not eliminate in places that people gathered and not disrupt anything or anyone while working in public was a challenge. If guide dogs, hearing dogs, or service dogs were not well-trained and went around intimidating or disrespecting people in social situations, their public access rights would be revoked as the lawmakers only agreed to having them exempt from companion dog laws for their training and the sole purpose of being used as a medical aid. Companion pet laws are in place because of the 99.8 percent of *what's in your dog*, not the 0.2 percent that makes it a pet.

The assistance dog work ethic, temperament, and job capitalizes on the 0.2 percent of the genes that we domesticated and neotenized and can easily be manipulated without harsh verbal or physical intervention, keeping the 99.8 percent wild within from ever surfacing. The stability it takes to remain calm and balanced while working in unpredictable public situations is not found in every dog. Only some dogs will qualify as having what it takes to do the job well. Assistance dogs must work throughout their lives, practicing their skills with a responsible guardian leading the way.

Just like herding and hunting or police dogs, not every dog is suited for this kind of work, where impulse control and problem-solving pose unique daily challenges that you are either suited for or not. An assistance dog must be very stable, submissive, flexible, and willing to follow and appease its leader with a puppy-like mentality but with the maturity, stability, and self-control of an adult. Not an easy combination to find.

Today, there are service dog programs around the world; thanks to Bonnie Bergin, who had the guts to persevere through adversity and live her dream awake! Because she knew her vision of liberating lives, with the help of a canine companion, could radically change the life of a disabled person forever. Guide dogs had already proven that some forty years earlier when the first guide dog team was introduced in the United States. But the public and the laws in the 1970s only recognized guide dogs as being allowed to accompany their partners, where pets were not allowed. Bonnie Bergin and the original service dog users she placed dogs with had to fight hard to convince lawmakers that their service dog teams should have the same public access rights as guide dogs. These people did not fight for the pet owner's right to bring their pet where pets are not permitted.

Dogs Behaving Badly

Service Dogs for Self-Reliance in training.

Assistance dog teams seen working in public places are representing every other assistance dog team in the world. If an assistance dog eliminates in a store or growls at people who approach their handler, they are setting a terrible example for every other working dog. The federal law makes it clear that a person with a disability *can and should* be asked to remove his service animal from the premises if:

1. The animal is out of control and the animal's owner does not take action to control the dog. For example, a dog that barks repeatedly and makes unwelcome contact with people or keeps whining, and so on.
2. The animal poses a direct threat to the health or safety of others. For example, eliminating indoors, sniffing at food in grocery stores or restaurants, growling, lunging, and so on.

An assistance dog *must* be able to work as a nonintrusive helpmate. It is the dog's responsibility to not get in people's way when working. The dog has no rights. The person is the one with the rights. If a dog is a nuisance in public, it can't be an assistance dog. People are not obligated to put up with any assistance animal's poor training. That's the law. A business has the right to tell a disabled person that they can enjoy their establishment, but their dog can no longer accompany them if it causes disturbances the disabled person can't control. The general public and businesses have a right to not have to alter the way they do things, just to accommodate an unqualified, poorly behaved assistance dog.

Service Dog Trainer and User Etiquette

1. Train your dog to eliminate on command and always give your dog an opportunity to eliminate before entering any public space.
2. Carry at least two cleanup kits with you at all times when working in public places and always pick up after your dog.
3. Never allow your assistance dog to ride in a shopping cart. Microscopic diseases are no joke. I don't want a dog in my grocery cart. Do you? In fact, parents are already being warned of how unsanitary shopping carts are for their kids as it is. Let's not add to the germs.
4. If you cannot control your service dog in a public place, it is your responsibility to remove the dog immediately.
5. Train your dog to not groom itself in public places. Scratching and body shaking leaves hair behind, and licking is never acceptable in public. It's kind of like picking your nose. You might really want to but etiquette says don't do it in public.

Reality Check

There are important things to consider before deciding to train your own service dog. *All service dog trainers must* be able to separate themselves from believing that the dog they are training *will* become a service dog. You may spend thousands of dollars in purchasing the "right dog," buying food, accessories, paying for vet bills, and spending a whole year of your time and effort in training and bonding with your dog only to have to release it as a pet because its temperament is not suitable to work in public places.

All your time, effort, and good intentions do not guarantee that you'll have a legitimate, well-trained service dog. Even if you do put two years of training into it, the success rate in the world's top service dog agencies is low, an average of four out of ten dogs trained actually become official service dogs that continue to work once placed. And these are the top professionals in the world, so your chances of breeding or choosing the right dog are risky. It's a battle Bonnie Bergin has tried to win since the service dog's earliest beginning. And although the success rate has improved dramatically over the years, there are still long waiting lists of people needing a dog to help liberate their lives.

Rescued from a shelter, owner trained service dog Sammy has the right temperament for the job; as he enjoys another adventure with Michelle and Sammy's partner Steve.

If you can admit to yourself that your dog may not have the right temperament for the job, then *you are ready* to become a service dog trainer. If you *are not willing to face the fact* that a service dog is not a pet but a respectable member of a larger group of assistance dogs around the world, then *you are not ready* to train your own dog and should seek out a trained service dog to be placed with. Training a real legitimate service animal is advanced work and is not as easy as you may think. But it is also not impossible if you educate yourself and continue to be a responsible trainer and user. *Pets are not service dogs. No matter how good they make you feel.*

CHAPTER 5

Who Are You?

WHO YOU ARE and how you interact on a daily basis with your dog will determine what kind of leadership style you represent and what kind of feedback your dog will give you in return. If you are overly assertive, impatient, or use intimidation to train and raise your dog's skill level, it might make you feel powerful and get you results, but it also makes you feel stressed out, which sends a message to the dog that you are an unconfident, unbalanced, hostile, and unpredictable leader that must be obeyed to avoid further conflict and keep himself or herself safe. While a dominant, confident dog might choose to challenge or fight you with disobedience or aggression if feeling threatened, other domestic dogs might submit with appeasement, fear, or avoidance behaviors to cope.

Like its cousin the wolf, your pet has no choice but to take rank somewhere in its pack. Remember the alpha and omega wolf? Sadly, dogs are the only predator, I know of, that can be abused and will continue to try to please you in hopes of gaining a higher rank and eventually become a more stable member of the family pack. Or tragically, sometimes they will attack their leader to subdue and control him to take his leadership and regain balance. If it's a five-pound aggressive Chihuahua that attacks its owner, you never hear about it, but if it's a sixty-pound pit bull, it makes the headlines, and the dog is blamed for being a killer breed. What's in you manifests itself in your dog. The 0.2 percent of the dog's genes that is domestic in our pets is only available to us if we tap into it to activate and use it to our advantage. Otherwise, your dog will use that 0.2 percent and the 99.8 percent of itself to manipulate you since he knows what you're thinking and feeling about him and yourself at all times.

If you are too docile of a leader, however, the dog will take advantage of you by challenging or taking over your leadership to keep you both safe from your own instability. This is why having a dog that's a little less dominant than you, with a personality and energy level that matches yours, is so important. An introvert person with an extrovert dog will always be out of sync compared to the introvert person with the introvert dog, who is more natural together.

The introvert person with the extrovert dog will only work well together if the dog is worked someway. For example, there are lots of introverts who are active in search and rescue and agility with their pets, and they need an extrovert dog for a job or sport like that. Introverts might like watching their dog play at the dog park or enjoy sending them to a good doggy day care to give them an extrovert outlet so they can enjoy their downtime when they are with their introvert owners since the dog still gets to stimulate its personal need to be social, even though you might not be.

Introverts are not all shy, antisocial, or homebodies, like we might think. Many people (including me) live vicariously through their dogs. It's a way to socialize without the focus being on the introvert person. They can enjoy being around extroverts through their dog's social activities. Every person and dog needs an outlet to express who they really are in order for them to feel balanced, in sync, and accepted in any social group. Mother Nature has created a whole range of different personality types in all social animals so they must come together to find a balance—often depending on the strengths of others to help us succeed where we might fail.

It all comes down to *who you are and what you got a dog for?* If it's just a showpiece with no real purpose, then you

GOOD PUPPY ACADEMICS

better have gotten a dog that doesn't mind being one. Older dogs or breeds like the Pug, Chihuahua, or Greyhound and many introvert dogs often enjoy being coddled, pampered, and homebodies. But they still need you to give them what they need to stay balanced. If they are unhappy, living with them will become a stress. If their needs are fulfilled, then you will both be in sync and happy living together. There are always ways to make it work if you put the time and effort it takes to make it happen.

You must guide the training in a confident and controlled way without having to force your subject to cooperate while adding the right amount of love and affection into the mix. Remember, your dog is trapped between 0.2 percent of what we want and 99.8 percent of what its nature wants. Building a trusting, secure bond will allow the dog to decide you are worthy of being followed since your discipline is recognized as a learning experience not as a control issue. A good leader controls his followers with incentives that satisfy their innate desire to cooperate since their efforts are reinforced with pleasurable and rewarding consequences. But that does not mean there are not any negative consequences sprinkled into the lessons as that's nature's way and we call it operant conditioning, remember?

As we began to domesticate wolves, our ancient ancestors selected the offspring that were less likely to turn on them later in their adult lives and make a meal of them, especially since the average wolf is a very large animal weighing at least a hundred and twenty pounds or more in adulthood. So breeding and selecting for the most docile temperament was critical to our own survival. We learned how to care for wolves by watching wolves and incorporating what works with our own young. But as we know, 99.8 percent of the dog's thinking is set by nature, while only 0.2 percent belongs to us primates. Primate and canine etiquette and social interactions are not the same, and you will never convince your dog that a primate knows best since they know us better than we know them.

Our primate nature allowed us to raise young pups with the same parental attention we would indulge on our own young, but the relationship had to remain in balance since these domesticated wolves would recognize human weakness, which could trigger their primal need to protect themselves by taking over leadership. Remember, the wolf was not domesticated to be a burden to us. It was to utilize their deadly innate talents in the hunt that really drew us to them at first. Early humans with well-trained hunting dogs were much safer and ate better than those without them.

Unlike our own toddlers, a dog's fight, flight, avoidance, and submission responses are hardwired and developed very early on in their lives since 99.8 percent of their genetics drives their nature. The 0.2 percent we tamed did not remove this innate survival mechanism. All it did was dull it enough for us to manipulate it easier. *Nature and nurture* helped us to mold the domestic dog into what it is today. But the human leader must lead like another dog would not like he would with his human children. When treated like a human (primate) child, a dog will become confused and start exhibiting behaviors that are consistent with feeling vulnerable, imbalanced, or confused by your input. These behaviors can manifest into fight, flight, submission, and avoidance responses or even excitement, anxiety, fear, and aggression.

For example, greeting your human children when you get home at the door with hugs and excitement is a normal, balanced way humans communicate with each other. We do the same during the holidays with friends and relatives. It's a good etiquette to recognize and welcome someone this way. It shows them how much you appreciate their company. But transfer this human etiquette mentality to your dog, greeting you at the door and the excitement looks more like an out of

GOOD PUPPY ACADEMICS

control pee fest with jumping, scratching, nipping, and biting instead of kisses and hugs.

Or sharing your meal with your dog as you would if someone saw you eating something good and took an interest in it, Homo Saipan etiquette says to offer them a piece, to where the canine etiquette says to gobble it up as fast as you can before someone sees it and wants a piece. With the exception of their young or their mates, predators don't usually share with other predators of another species or even with their own kind. They merely tolerate each other so everyone gets to eat.

Although rarely documented, if intimidation doesn't work, bears and lone wolves will sometimes tolerate each other (operant conditioning) over eating a large kill if everyone is really hungry (classical conditioning), and the bear knows he is not in danger and can still eat enough as long as he lets the wolf have a little too. Foxes and wolverines have been documented using teamwork to hunt, and although not the norm, these anomalies do occur in nature. Animals who are opportunists get rewarded often. But they also face greater risks to achieve their success.

Remember the rule of survival says to take care of your own self-interests first, or you could end up dead. The will to live another day and pass on your genes and raise young is what drives them all. Once that drive is no longer their motivation, they are on the downward spiral to eventual death. Wild predators have to grow up and reproduce in approximately one-fifth the time a human being has since they have an average life span of ten to twenty years in the wild or less depending on the animal and its circumstances.

Caution! Beautiful Kiki knows how to use her eyes to melt your heart. Even I have trouble resisting that face!

Then there are the times when your dog looks at your steak dinner with those pouty eyes and that feel bad for me look, what he is really saying is that he wants to have a piece of your "kill." The dog will often use the puppy mentality approach and give appeasement behaviors to trigger a nurturing response from you, just like a wolf puppy would do to encourage adults to nurture and feed it. The 0.2 percent part of the genes we manipulated and conditioned recognizes that humans respond to these signals as well.

Then there are the ones who just jump the table or your plate and take their chances of stealing your steak with excitement or aggression driving their behavior, like an impulse-driven adolescent, since the 99.8 percent nature of the dog invites it to take advantage of this easy meal before

GOOD PUPPY ACADEMICS

the human (other predator) eats it all. If your dog is lying down quietly at a distance watching you eat, he is practicing good predator etiquette; submissive animals often wait and watch and then scavenge on whatever the other predator leaves behind.

Your ability to claim and protect your meal (kill) and have your dog greet you with respect at the door makes you very powerful in your dog's eyes. Your dog doesn't need to know how to sit, lie down, or walk nicely on the leash to see you as its leader. Those things allow you to have control over your dog in a different, less primitive way. Sharing food with your dog is part of the primitive, social bonding experience, but begging and stealing makes your dog the more powerful one in the relationship, not you. This is why I tell all my pet parents that the treat (kill) is a reward for the correct behavior (skill). So the golden rule with treat training is always no skill no kill. Since Mother Nature doesn't give handouts.

Because I work with the general public and know people feed their dogs people food out of guilt, instead of just telling them not to, I like to give them insight as to how to do this like a dog instead of like a human. You can accomplish the food-sharing bond with your dog as long as you control it but never off your food plate unless you are willing to make your dog wait patiently without begging for it. However, in doing this, you are actually elevating your dog's rank in his mind since you are still allowing him to be near you, anticipating a bite of your meal. So *it's really not a good idea.*

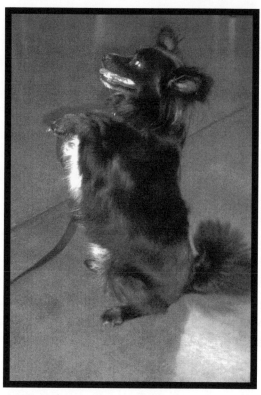

Rupert loves using his cute tricks to get what he wants.

Instead, having him lay ten feet away from you and wait calmly, patiently, and quietly while you are consuming your meal, then inviting him to have some when you are done, in his own bowl away from the table, upholds his lower rank as a submissive member that must wait respectfully for the leader to say, "I'm done you can scavenge what's leftover now." You could also give him canned dog food or just a dog treat instead of human food if you prefer. It doesn't have to be at your mealtime. If you don't want your dog near the table, then don't allow it. *You set the rules remember*. And never give your dog fast food and other processed human food as it's not even healthy for human consumption, let alone your dogs. Stick with natural foods. But *keep in mind dogs do not process some food the same way we do* and can become ill eating what we can without harmful effects.

A behavior you set and practice consistently is what it takes to be a successful and respected leader. People food such as some fruit, melon, veggies, skinless chicken, lean beef, rice, plain pasta, hard-boiled egg whites, and fat-free cottage cheese, for example, can be tolerated and enjoyed as a supplement to the diet of dogs that don't have special dietary needs. And some foods are downright dangerous like grapes, chocolate, and many other human foods can cause very bad side effects and should be avoided, so ask your veterinarian and educate yourself before feeding your pet anything new.

Your dog needs a balanced diet designed specifically for dogs, but supplementing with healthy dog treats or food for training sessions is a good way to enhance your bond with your pet. Whenever you feed your dog treats or a meal, they should be made to work for it in some way. A simple sit, stay, and release is much better than letting your dog get excited and rush the food bowl before it even touches the ground. Nobody rides for free. That's Mother Nature's way.

You do not have to share your meal with your pet if you don't want to, but if you do, you better be sending the right messages to your predator friend. If you just feed your dog his dog food supplemented with treats and the occasional chewstick or bone to enjoy, that works too. Just make your dog wait for your permission in a respectful and patient manner if he wants to have access to these high-value things.

When domestic dogs become tense, dominate, or aggressive around their toys, owners, water, or meal, they become very powerful and are a danger to other dogs and humans as the 99.8 percent predator within them emerges to guard its precious resource. Wolf puppies do this when young, while playing and eating with each other, as a way to practice establishing rank among their sibling pack and in their early juvenile stages together when they are still permitted to get away with it by the adults who feel no threat from their learning experiences.

But once they grow up and can hold their own as adults, this behavior becomes serious and can be deadly if the balance in the pack's pecking order gets challenged or changed. Pack dynamics are not set for life. They change as leaders lose their rank or die and new ones emerge. It is important to control this behavior, and all you have is your confident leadership and the 0.2 percent of domestication to work with, so you don't have many chances to keep failing at convincing your dog that you are not a competitor but an ally that he needs to cooperate with.

Adult Shepherd mix Rusty plays nicely with Bruno, a German Shepard mix puppy. Both have been taught good leash manners when interacting with each other.

A wolf puppy doesn't aggressively attack its adult packmates for rank. That happens when they are adults and have to hold their own. So don't allow this behavior to escalate, or the dog will be in control of you. Educate yourself on how to train your dog to not see you as a competitor using positive reinforcement as the motivator because that's really who you need to be in your dog's eyes. It's the science of learning, and you now know how it can work for or against you depending on how you use it.

Whatever the behavior is that you are training, always try using positive reinforcement first. If that's not working, choose from the appropriate alternatives such as removing the reward and ignoring the undesired behavior (negative punishment), substitute the behavior with another more desired one, remove the cause of the behavior, cue the behavior, change the association from an undesired one to a desired one, or, if necessary, add a quick humane correction (positive punishment) to get the dog's attention. But avoid the temptation of using negative reinforcement, or you could lose the dog's trust in you.

The Human and Canine Partnership

Dogs sense what you are thinking by your chemical scent and love to make you feel good by exhibiting puppy-like behaviors.

Domestic dogs often greet their human kin mouth-to-mouth as if they were submissive wolf pups greeting their adult pack members.

So who are you really? If you are like most of us, you think you know who you are, but how does your dog feel about you? What is the feedback you get when interacting with your pet? Is it stressful, or is it pleasurable? Or is it both? If it's both, then you are already halfway there. If it's stressful, you have a lot of work to do to gain some balance. Communication skills can help you manage your dog and allows you to control the way you interact with each other without stress dominating the situation, but knowing what drives your dog's behavior and how you influence it is the key to understanding how you can turn a situation around.

When you chose to take on the responsibility of being a canine guardian, you did not just become a new pet owner but you also became a dog handler, trainer, and psychologist. All three roles are important, and this is where your average old-school dog trainers and pet owners fall short. You can't just be a trainer *if you are living with your dog day in and day out.* As a trainer, I can't enforce a person's rule since I don't live with their dog. I can only show the pet owner how it's done through training, handling, and dog psychology, but the pet owner must understand how to apply it every day at home since I am not there to help them. A great trainer knows it's critical that the pet owner understands this. Training commands alone is not the answer. It's just part of the solution. The rest lies in the handling skills and knowing what your dog is thinking.

Helping you to become a confident and sensible leader is more than just showing you how to make your dog walk nicely on the leash, sit, or come when called. A dog trainer simply creates desired behaviors while a handler manages the dog, and a dog psychologist understands the science of the dog's mind and how to influence it. That's why it is important to find a qualified animal trainer to help you create the behaviors you want in your dog since the average dog trainer can only teach you skill development and knows little about dog psychology and neuroassociations, like you do now. You will know the difference between a great trainer and an average one by the way they have you treat your dog. Remember the Mary Poppins' analogy?

Miniature Pinscher Minnie loves being fashionable in her stylish shirts. The shirts help to keep her warm and her guardian says, "Minnie seems calmer when she wears them."

So always keep in mind how a *great* animal trainer uses all three skills to help you understand and train your dog. I was fortunate to have taken the path I took when getting my bachelor's degree to teach elementary schoolchildren. When I chose my elective classes, I specifically gravitated toward concentrations in human psychology and communication skills. My thought was that I needed to know how my subjects think if I was going to be effective at empowering them as a mentor. Not to mention, I figured my job would be much easier and less stressful if I knew what motivates and encourages my subjects to overcome challenging situations that can become roadblocks to learning.

What I learned from those classes in child psychology, development, and human communication was that I myself was never taught any of this in the first *twenty-five years* of my life! Boy was that an eye-opener. So I've spent the last thirty-two years perfecting what I learned to recondition myself and help others to do the same. This education was a rude awakening but has served me well, and I thank *nature and nurture* for helping to change my neuroassociations. I could never have done it alone. I had many mentors helping to cheer me on to be all that I could be and many stumbling blocks to overcome along the way as well.

So take a deeper look at who you really are. Are you defined by an occupation or your status in society? Do you feel rich, poor, happy, sad, content, or restless? Have you ever even thought about who you would be if all your values and treasures were no longer what defined you? Are you in balance with whom you are *in this modern world* and who you are by *nature*? Are you in touch with, and satisfied with, who you really are inside? How you answered these questions will determine what you may want or need to work on in your everyday existence to keep your life balanced in both realms, and your dog can help you to do that.

When Bonnie Bergin started placing service dogs with physically impaired individuals, one of the challenges was matching the recipient with a dog that would not challenge its handler or take advantage of their physical weakness as Bonnie's goal was always to move away from choke chains and having to teach behaviors by physically correcting or manipulating the dog. Not having to constantly manage the dog was important, so training for automatic behaviors was a must. Bonnie found that it took a very special temperament dog for this kind of work since the handler was obviously physically weak and the dog knew it. The handler needed a submissive dog to control it in public, using their voice and the dog's training alone. But a dog that was too submissive was often not stable enough to work as a service dog, so again, the right balance was important as training proved to not be the only solution to reaching Bonnie's ultimate goal. In the end, *it seemed that temperament was even more important.*

All dogs can be taught to work by voice command. But it takes a great deal of training and consistency to achieve it on a regular basis. From the sheep herding Border Collie to police dogs, who are trained to be controlled verbally by a confident stable leader, to the fearful, insecure, and anxious dog that is verbally abused to be controlled by an unbalanced human dictator, dogs respond to the training effort and energy you put out to determine if their fight, flight, avoidance, submission, or cooperation response should be utilized. So help them to make the cooperative decision with a willing confidence and trust in you rather than forcing your will on them.

Dogs are loyal and true to their most primitive selves. They aim to please and seek a balance within their environments. Cooperation is the norm for the canine and human species. Flexibility, endurance, and survival strategy are hardwired in both of us but in ways that are separated by our need to succeed in a world where our nature is often overridden by the demand to conform to a schedule that's out of sync with our natural biorhythms and a lifestyle dictated by what we can afford.

Dogs have not evolved with us; they have just been by our side during the process. The human and canine partnership has always been a symbiotic one. Human will would have never been able to tame the wild within the wolf. It took a partnership based on respect and an understanding that both parties could benefit from the relationship. So whether a pet or working dog, the same training standards apply when it comes to building a solid partnership that will last a lifetime.

GOOD PUPPY ACADEMICS

What Is an Rx Pharmdog?

Rx Pharmdog Jack grabs a pen to write your prescription to wellness.

Jack carefully writes your prescription. To be sure, he is bringing out the best in you.

After writing the prescription, Rx Pharmdog Jack recommends a good dose of daily dog activity coupled with love and affection endorphins to enhance the Pharmdog effect.

Rx Pharmdog is the term I coined to describe a dog that mitigates a person's mental disorder *by altering their brain chemistry* similar to a pharmaceutical drug. As a professional service dog trainer, I am well-versed in the laws. The federal law is clear about service dogs having to perform at least one physical task that helps to mitigate their partner's disability. It does not recognize dogs that just make you "feel good." But this "feel-good" phenomenon *that many people experience* from interacting with a dog has everything to do with the brain's chemicals such as oxytocin and cortisol affecting the body and mind as it reacts to this canine intervention. Dogs were changing people's state (neural pathways) of mental health *long before we called them service dogs*. It is why we have kept different animals as pets for as long as we have been interested in the animals around us and had the means to feed and care for them. Villagers have kept small monkeys, birds, and other cute wild critters as pets for thousands of years, just to enjoy them simply, because they make you feel good when you interact with them, without having to take the risk of being preyed on by them since these types of animals are not a life-threatening danger to people. But unlike these harmless, undomesticated monkeys and birds, *the wolf had to be domesticated first* before we could safely enjoy the mental health benefits of the dog as we know it today.

Bonnie Bergin saw how, by simply adding a dog to the mix, *a disabled person's state of mental health improved* as the dog performed physical tasks that were vital to their independence. People who had depression due to their physical limitations became alive again with a canine companion unconditionally there by their side. They could be physically independent and actually attract people in social setting, instead of feeling invisible, using the service dog as a social bridge to close the gap between them and the able-bodied community who often feel uncomfortable speaking to someone in a wheelchair or with a disability.

Ask any service dog user and they will tell you that the mental health benefits of having a task-trained service dog often outweigh the tasks that they perform. There have been many studies over the years proving that animal therapy is real. But it's seen just like the placebo effect. Somehow, western medicine has totally missed the boat on how powerful the mind really is. I assume that's partly because it's not something the pharmaceutical industry likes to hear since they know all about controlling brain chemicals.

More and more doctors, therapists, and psychiatrists are beginning to "prescribe" (so to speak) dogs for their patients as they too have finally recognized the psychological effects that Bonnie Bergin realized dogs provide for the disabled long ago. But according to the law, these dogs are not legitimate service dogs unless they perform a physical task to mitigate the person's disorder or disability. Here is why I call these types of dogs Rx Pharmdogs.

According to the American Heritage Online Dictionary, the definition of Rx (ar'eks') is:

1. a prescription for medicine or a medical appliance
2. a remedy, cure, or solution for a disorder or problem.

When prescribed by a therapist or doctor as a remedy, cure, or solution for a disorder or problem, these dogs should also be considered service dogs. It is my belief that if a dog's intervention triggers chemical changes in the brain that causes positive improvements to a person's state of mental health and well-being, an Rx pharmdog should be considered a vital part of the person's wellness plan, just like pharmaceuticals and group therapy are. And in the eyes of the law, an assistance dog is already seen as a medical appliance.

Severe cases of mental instabilities like posttraumatic stress disorder, depression, anxiety, bipolar disorder, and other mental health issues often go unnoticed by others. It can be a silent suffering that a person learns to live with just to survive. Psychotherapy can help a lot, and medications can be lifesaving, but feeling consumed by your illness when you are alone leaves you feeling empty, and no medication or therapy can fill in the loneliness you feel day in and day out. Being unconditionally accepted and loved is a human need. When we don't have a proper balance of it, we fail to be whole and thrive.

For someone who has lost their trust in people or has no faith in themselves, it's often impossible to change their minds about other people and situations, but a dog is unbiased and has no motives other than to live and let live. When the right dog is matched with the right person, wellness can happen. Task training like waking a medicated person up at certain times or to take their medication and getting them out of the house can change a person's neuroassociations much faster than a person waking you up every day and nagging at you to get up, take your meds, and do something with your life because *there are some things only a dog can achieve when human intervention fails.*

Unfortunately, people are already taking advantage of service dog laws by taking pets where they are not permitted to go. So task training is the only way to define the legalities of what makes a service dog different than a pet. Pet owners need to unite to change the laws or quit bringing their pets where the law says they can't go in order to not jeopardize the rights of those who need a dog to accompany them due to a legitimate disability that the dog helps mitigate. I wish that all *responsible dog owners* and their *well-behaved pets* could accompany them wherever they go. I think they deserve to have the privilege if they are responsible handlers and their dogs are well-behaved. But the liability of having irresponsible owners bringing their unsuited, untrained, and misbehaved dog in public places is too high, not to mention the mess dogs make that many of their owners leave behind.

CHAPTER 6

Frequently Asked Training Questions

Cute *Cairn Terrier* Clara.

Q: What kind of training equipment will I need to train my new dog or puppy?

A: The equipment needed will depend on the dog at first. Since a puppy will grow very fast over the first ten months, don't invest a lot of money on things like collars and leashes as they are all temporary for now. A simple collar and a four-foot long leash is all you need at first. I also recommend a material (with chain link) martingale (no slip) collar for training or an easy walk harness that connects the leash to the front of the dog's chest if you find that the dog or puppy pulls when learning to walk on a loose leash. All dogs must have good leash manners. They should be taught to walk in both the heel position and if needed a loose leash walk without having tension on the leash. A dog must learn to loosen the tension on the leash automatically whenever he feels it tighten so the handler can use their arms when needed without being impeded by the dog at the end of the leash. A good trainer can help you decide which equipment to use on your dog and show you how to accomplish this in a productive way.

Q: What are *your criteria* for training a service dog?

A: I believe that all dogs should respond and work primarily by voice command. The leash should not have to be used to control any dog, especially not a service dog. The leash is necessary because many dogs are unpredictable and impulsive. Dogs are like small children they do not reason. They just react with instinct unless well-trained and supervised. This is why having the right dog working in public places is critical. Whether it's a service dog or a police dog, the more stable and even tempered a dog is, the less likely it is to become unstable in stressful situations. This is where it comes down to temperament and not just training. If your service dog must be managed with the leash all the time, then it needs more training *in my opinion*.

I see service dogs working with head harnesses all the time. Some of the top service dog training agencies in the world have switched to using them to train every dog they place. Even young puppies are made to wear them from the very beginning of their training. The original domestic dogs and the first domesticated wolves were not trained this way as leashes were not traditionally used in the dog's fifteen-thousand year history. Most dogs living in the world today never wear a leash. It is only in societies like ours where they are required by law. Leashes are not natural. But audio and visual signal control is. The leash only serves two purposes. It keeps your untrained dog safe from all the hazards mankind has put in the environment, and the law says you must have it, but it's not how you should have control of your dog.

A group of service dogs in advanced training practice their sit, stay for the camera and off leash reliability while taking a romp on the beach, a great way to exercise and train at the same time.

The face halter, or halti, was not available in 1975 when Bonnie Bergin introduced the service dog concept. It was pretty much choke chains and prong collars back then since a lot of traditional dog trainer's mentality was to control the dog through rote training methods and physically forcing their will on their subjects to gain results. Bonnie Bergin's idea for a service dog was never about "controlling" the dog. It has always been about having a symbiotic partnership, where the service dog actually became an extension of their human partner willingly working as their partners in mobility.

It took a combination of understanding the dog's mind and natural inclinations through the eyes of a dog and the science of how learning theory works to eventually find the right balance. By the 1990s, Bonnie was seriously inclined to not use any choke chains or other equipment that was viewed as inhumane in the public's eyes. Instead, she focused her attention on choosing the dog that could work without these tools. Less service dogs make the grade this way, and this became a problem for Bonnie, but it was always Bonnie Bergin's intention to have a dog that can function well without the use of special equipment to manage them. Today, Bonnie's working dogs work without this equipment, so not as many dogs get placed as full service dogs, but that's what makes her service dogs unique and different. Other service dog programs around the world have taken on her approach as new students graduate from her university and open their own assistance dog programs.

But the types of dogs who are naturally inclined for doing this type of work with or without hard-core training are probably one in ten dogs if even that. Bonnie happened to hit on the right dog on her first try with Abdul, but it was all trial and error for years in the beginning. However, in saying this, the *demand for service dogs in the world is so high* that if service dog agencies depended on breeding or finding that perfect dog that can work by voice command while ignoring environmental distractions, the demand would never be met, and countless people with disabilities would not have the opportunity to be independent with the use of a service dog. Not to mention having the mental health benefits the dog brings to the relationship.

So *my personal preference* is in having, and training, a service dog with the temperament to do the job willingly, reliably, and automatically without the use of equipment to control them. Think about it. A quadriplegic cannot be expected to use any equipment to control their dog. The first people Bonnie Bergin set out to help were those with very limited mobility. Abdul was literally the hands, arms, and legs of Kerry Knaus, the world's first service dog user.

Wheelchair bound, Kerry's disability made her severely immobile, so she and Bonnie created the behaviors and commands used by many service dog teams today. This enabled Kerry the freedom to not have to wait for human intervention when she needed a helping hand, giving her greater independence by allowing her to handle a dog that she could not physically control. The partnership wasn't perfect by any means, but it was a step in the right direction that has brought us to where we are today.

Do I think these service dogs are well-trained? Yes, no doubt about it! The ones who don't do their jobs well are not placed as service dogs or pulled from working if they do not uphold the necessary standards after placement. Dogs love helping people. That's the whole idea. The top agencies in the world have great concern for the liability associated with putting out a poor quality helpmate. They, of all people, are the ones who drive the laws that give you the privilege of using an assistance dog. It is a serious business, and the respectable programs follow the guidelines of the laws they helped to create.

Training equipment all has its purpose when used correctly on the right dog for the right reasons. If you have tried positive reinforcement and your large dog is still out of control and can physically harm you or someone else or a dog's attention cannot be redirected on walks, making it impossible to train him, *then I recommend* the holt or halti brand face halter. I never recommend pinch collars since they work well on submissive dogs, which feel the pain and don't want to keep being punished, so this dog really just needs an easy walk harness or face halter and a confident trainer to lead it. Since pain is not a pleasurable way to learn how to enjoy your walks. Using a face halter on a dog or puppy as a shortcut to train the brain however, is not a good way to set neuroassociations *in my experience*. Self-control isn't learned that way.

Then there is the assertive, dominant dog that keeps pulling anyway, allowing the pinch collar to continuously pinch its neck, and becomes more agitated, never getting anything but pain and frustration during its outings, while building negative associations every time they go out in public. Bully breeds and terriers can react aggressively to the pain of something biting at their neck all the time and redirect this frustration onto others in their environment.

Pinch collars have their place, but not many trainers or pet owners know which dogs they are effective and necessary to have on or how to use them properly. They are often used by trainers and pet owners who use this tool as a shortcut to not have to put in the time it takes to teach (recondition) the dog to walk properly on the leash. Same goes for the choke chain. The martingale collar, easy walk harness, and face halter are much better choices for the average pet owner and their dog, along with the proper training from a great trainer who can show you how to properly train your dog to walk without pulling versus controlling your dog with this equipment.

Q: How can I tell if I am more dominant than my dog?

A: Before I start using the term *dominant*, I'd like to clarify *what I intend* it to mean. I use the word *dominant* to describe a dog that is one or a combination of the following traits: pushy, bossy, and usually competitive. I *never* use the word *dominant* to describe aggression. I will use the word *aggression* to describe the behavior. Submissive dogs that are fearful can often be the worst cases of aggression. So like submission, dominance is not an aggressive behavior. Simply put, *a dominant person or dog sees themselves as being in charge.* So if you are in charge, then you are more dominating than your dog. For example, a fearful dog that runs and has you chase it and then hides under the bed where you can't get to it has just dominated the situation, to where a confident dog might choose to directly challenge you by disobeying to dominate the situation or, in the worst-case scenario, attack you to remain in control.

This is why you must get a dog with the right temperament for your comfort level. The closer you two are in personality and energy level, the easier it will be for you to manage your dog. If you are a very passive person or an overdominant one, you will know it by the feedback your dog speaks to you in his body language and actions.

Remember, a very confident, high strung, extrovert personality Labrador retriever with his nose to the ground, which comes from a long line of hunting genes, might make a great hunting dog but may not make the best service dog or pet. But the same line can also produce a sibling or two, who are more submissive, calm, and easygoing that won't make good hunters. This makes a better pet or service dog for someone who needs a more submissive and relaxed dog to live with. It's just like how wolves were selected way back fifteen thousand years ago. *They were selected for how they could help us.* Not for how we can help them. Early man was not interested in dogs who were not good hunters or herders since pet dogs were often a burden to feed and care for.

GOOD PUPPY ACADEMICS

Buyer Beware

Puppies can win someone over easily with their adorable behaviors but buyer beware. Is this the right dog for you?

There are so many unknowledgeable or irresponsible people breeding dogs without any understanding or concern for the temperament or health of the puppies. You must do your research and choose the right dog according to *the standards you expect* from the breeder all the way to the dog. Rescues and shelters are also a resource for finding the right dog, and they often don't know anything about the dog's background.

I have seen great dogs come from these resources (including mine), and dogs whose health or temperament were less stable. Even getting a dog from a responsible breeder that is breeding for health and temperament isn't guaranteed. Remember, that in every litter or rescue, there is always more than one personality type to choose from, and as for genetic soundness, that's something that is never guaranteed. This is why it's important to at least know more about different traits and what you are and aren't looking for in a dog.

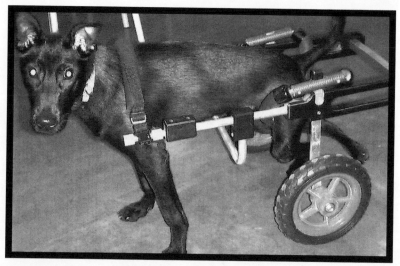

Rescued from Taiwan, this pup's back legs are deformed from a genetic defect. Happy and full of life on the front end, this wheelchair device allows her to move around like other dogs.

There are countless dogs and puppies looking for homes around the world. Rescue groups in the United States are helping to save dogs from other countries these days as more countries trap and eliminate strays that have no one to love and care for them. Our shelters here are full of dogs being euthanized on a daily basis as well. The sad thing is that these shelters never intended to kill animals when they originally set up shop years ago. They were set up to save animals and help them. It is the general population's irresponsibility that causes these shelters to overflow with unwanted animals. And we blame them for their cruelties so not to have to look at ourselves.

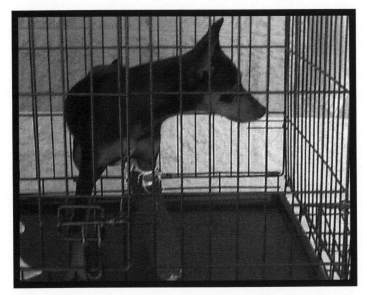

This purebred *Miniature Pinscher* ended up at a rescue with a broken leg. People give up injured dogs they can't afford. Dogs will get euthanized if someone won't pay for medical care.

Every living thing on this planet deserves to be here. It is the most awesome place in the universe, and we've filled it with a lot of human garbage. But that can't change nature's beauty; it can only distract us from it. Dogs with genetic issues like skin ailments or physical deformities still deserve to have love and security in this world for however long they are here. We are their guardians, and we have become kin. They have no place in the natural world, except with us. We created freaks when we domesticated the wolf. Dogs cannot survive as wild animals and thrive. When they try, they become dangerous packs that roam the streets and get in trouble with society, a death sentence for many.

This irresistible face is no reason to rescue a dog. A puppy will require guidance from you that you may not be prepared to give. So think twice before being impulsive.

So if you adopt any dog, adopt it for the right reasons. Never adopt simply because you feel sorry or because you think the dog is cute. Look deeper than that because a dog is a lifelong commitment and they can never take care of themselves. Have a dog for the right reasons or don't have one at all.

If you must rehome your dog for any reason, find it a home better than what you could have provided for it, and you will never have to wonder if you failed your dog by putting it in an unstable situation for the rest of its life. Remember, dogs are stuck with what they get. They depend on your judgment, so be responsible when having to rehome your beloved pet whether you like the animal or not. So do the right thing. Someone out there is willing to love and care for it properly.

These two happy, healthy old dogs ended up in a shelter as a pair. When someone dies, their pets often end up euthanized if no one wants them. Lucky for these two as they were rescued.

There are people who take on one-legged dogs, old dogs, or even sick dogs to nurse back to health. All dogs can find a place. Unfortunately, some dogs will be euthanized if their quality of life will be painful or chronically stressful due to medical conditions or severe behavioral anomalies. Animals don't deserve to stay here to suffer either. It's a balance we are responsible for keeping as their creators and guardians.

Try walking in their paws for one day, and you would see how helpless a dog really is in this world. It's not their world they live in. Their world is our world. And if our world is out of balance, then so becomes theirs. So buyer beware, *don't make the purchase if you can't make the lifelong commitment.*

CHAPTER 7

Amazing Canines

Xiana dreams of being able to drive. If only her feet could reach those peddles!

OVER THE PAST fifteen years, service dogs and pets have inspired and taught me phenomenal things about the true capacity of the domestic dog. I never stop learning from the canine subjects I mentor as they continue to accompany us while we evolve as a species, looking for the next opportunity to teach us something new about us through them. Dogs often do things we think are so amazing. But just like those behaviors we hate, the behaviors we love most about the domestic dog also come from that 99.8 percent of their nature that we never altered since the 0.2 percent we genetically manipulated was all based on *our survival,* not theirs.

We took the kill out of the wolf and chose to nurture the gene pool that Mother Nature would have eliminated since they can't survive in our human society nature's way and endanger the population. Affection, loyalty, and the bond that creates a wolf pack's ties helped to connect our two species; since these traits resemble our own family structures. A balance was able to be naturally achieved as long as the human was not preyed upon by "his own kin."

Without the domestic dog, we would not be who we are today. Countless dogs have risked their lives for their own counties. War dogs are credited for saving countless soldiers' lives from having tragic endings due to their noble acts of loyalty. Border patrol dogs have had cartel hits placed on them due to their uncanny ability to outwit the human drug trafficker and stop the flow of dangerous drugs entering our country—explosive detection, and avalanche rescue dogs, perform important tasks that protect us. Search and rescue dogs make it possible for us to help each other more efficiently. Without them, life for us would be much different.

Toni and Toby visit patients at a local hospital as part of their weekly ritual. They both enjoy it because there are some things only a dog can do when human intervention fails.

Therapy dogs, Isabella and Cinnamon, love to do tricks for the people they visit. Dog's love helping people feel good. They sense the good chemical state they put you in when interacting.

Therapy dogs work with people who can benefit from their unique abilities to bring out the best in us. A smile goes a long way when you see how your pet can affect someone else's state of well-being. Sharing this gift with those who need a break from whatever situation might be causing them stress or depression sends feel-good chemicals rushing through a person's system. Neural associations of this kind are priceless, and you have the power to let your dog shine in this way through social therapy visits in critical care facilities, hospitals, independent living communities, and other places where people would enjoy a visit from a special dog. That's the *pharmdog* effect, and it is powerful.

GOOD PUPPY ACADEMICS

I was recently privileged to meet and work with an amazing dog that really went beyond what we would consider the norm for an average pet. This stray dog's remarkable deeds made a lot of people take notice of him. I highlight his story for you to appreciate the beauty that's in all dogs as I can't think of a better way to bring this book to a close.

Every dog has a unique quality that makes them special for who they are, but most pets never get to shine to their fullest potential due to lack of opportunity. I was fortunate enough to be part of this hero's journey as articulated by the woman named Ana, who took pity on a poor dog's plight and started a chain reaction that gave an unwanted, uncared for, street dog the opportunity to shine and help others in return, reaching his fullest potential thanks to a network of caring people who gave him a chance to shine. Here is his story.

A Hero's Story

Hero before a bath and shave. He was fluffy and matted after living on the streets for over six months.

I started a new job back in July 2011 at a day center next to Slonaker Elementary in San Jose, California. On the first morning that I started, I came across a small shaggy cream and whitish little dog; he was enjoying the morning sun, soon after more little dogs joined him. I'm told that they lived under a dumpster at the elementary school next to the day care but also hung out at the day care center.

I would see them every morning sunbathing; then the shaggy dog would get up and disappear while the other homeless dogs stayed and played in the school field. After a few hours, the shaggy dog would show up with unopened trash bags; then all these little homeless Chihuahua mixes would get so excited and would run toward this shaggy dog, who would rip open the plastic bags and let them look for food in the trash. He would sit patiently until they were finished; then he would look through it too. If there was nothing left, he would disappear again and come back with more trash bags. I was told by the neighbors that he would walk long distances to look for food and that he had been seen at two Mexican supermarkets located each at opposite ends of the neighborhood.

He would even look for water. It was funny and sad; at the same time, he would be looking in the field with all the other stray doggies behind him in a line. When he would locate a puddle of dirty water, he would drink so the other dogs could see that it was water, and then all the others would start drinking. I saw the shaggy dog playing with the neighborhood kids and how gentle he was with them; I saw how he played with all the other dogs and ran through the school field. I saw how he grew and got chunky from all the junk food he ate, even though that did not slow him down. He had doggies depending on him. I was amazed by the strength of this gorgeous dog with sweet big eyes that melt anyone's heart. After a couple of months, I tried to get close to him;

he looked at me with those beautiful eyes of his and turned around and left.

I was so busy at work, and with so many issues at home, I couldn't think of a way to help these dogs. Animal services was called numerous times to no avail. It was a joy to see the way this shaggy dog took care of the others and how the other doggies would rely on him and follow him. One time, a trash can was put on a picnic table and out of the reach of the dogs. The shaggy dog walked toward the table, and all the others followed. He then tried to knock down the trash can; meanwhile, all the others waited in a circle around him. He fights and has a hard time knocking it down, but he never gave up. When he finally knocks it over, all the doggies start looking for food. When he'd gotten tired, he would lie down, and all the other dogs would sit beside him; some of them would look for shelter under his belly when it got colder.

One day, I realized that one of the dogs is pregnant. I was so worried and asked for help on craigslist and called animal services again, but nothing happened. I was so immersed with work; that months passed by, and fall was already here, and the puppies were already one-month-old. I was afraid that those puppies were going to die out in cold, living under the dumpster, so I went to check on them. The shaggy dog was keeping them warm as well as their mom; he was wrapping himself around them. Mama dog started barking, and I backed away. Mama dog only left her puppies' side when food arrived; she took them out once in a while to play with them.

Once again, I asked for help in craigslist; I received many offers, but almost all of them were for the puppies. The only honest reply that I received was from a woman named Michele. Through her, I was contacted by Noah's B'Ark rescue in Santa Rosa, California, and they promptly agreed to take all the dogs. Michele contacted me immediately, and on December 14, 2011, she went to the day care and was able to catch mom, pups, and one small dog. Michele was surprised by the number of dogs living under the dumpster, but she did not see the shaggy guy.

On Saturday morning, December 17, I went to the day care to see if I can catch any more dogs. As I was arriving, I saw the shaggy dog with another dog, coming from down the street. This time, I had bags of treats, food, and water. I opened a bag of treats and started feeding them; they gently took the treats from me but did not let me pet them. To my surprise, this shaggy boy had tags, so I was able to get the phone number and called his owner; a lady answered the phone, and I asked her if she had lost her dog and let her know that he is in front of me.

She said that they had adopted him from a shelter, but he ran away a few days after, and that on one occasion, she tried to catch him, but he ran, and then one other time, she sent a neighbor, and he run away from him too. I couldn't understand. They lived a couple of streets away from the day care, and they never cared to bring him water, food or to win him over. I asked her if they had abused him; then silence, after a few seconds, she said, "Not that I know of." I had just given him some treats, and he got close to me; he was gentle and sweet; he was amazing, and she said that she did not want to go and get him! I got upset and said good-bye!

By then the shaggy little dog had already stolen the sealed bag of treats and had taken them inside the day care center, so I couldn't get to it. He ripped it open and shared the treats with the other dogs. I was so heartbroken; how can someone not want this amazing dog? That same afternoon, I went back to the day care, but sadly, none of the dogs was around; then I turned around and saw the shaggy dog and a "Foxy" looking female dog coming from down the street. I got excited and started calling them, and they started running really fast toward me. Finally, the shaggy little dog let me pet him, and then I hugged him and did not want to let go; I put him in my

GOOD PUPPY ACADEMICS

car and went back for the Foxy dog; she was there, but she was very afraid and skittish.

I drove back home and gave this dog a bath. I feel so moved by him. I just want to hug and kiss him and let him know that he could trust me. I have two dogs, and they are very territorial—the female sleeps with my nephew, and the male sleeps with us. Blue started barking incessantly at the shaggy dog, but the shaggy dog did not bark back, not even once. I feel so sorry for this dog. I spent the next couple of hours hugging the shaggy dog, trying to make him comfortable, and he looked at me like asking, "Do you really love me?" I couldn't look into his eyes because the next day I had to drive him to the rescue. I felt sad because I was not the one and I was not his forever home but also excited because he would have the opportunity to find a great forever home through Noah's B'Ark rescue.

Sunday morning, before driving to Santa Rosa, we go back to the day care to see if we could catch the Foxy dog but did not see any dogs, but as soon as I get the shaggy little dog out of my car, the stray dogs came out from hiding, even one injured dog that I had not seen in several days came out. A lady that lives next to the day care was out for a walk, and she asked me if I'm taking the shaggy dog, which I responded that I was taking him to a rescue. She told me that the shaggy dog had been caring for the injured dog that was run over by a car, and since I had taken the shaggy dog away, he had been forced to look for food on his own. The lady said she would see the shaggy dog taking trash bags under the dumpster that were most likely for that injured dog and that they had seen him since and he had gotten better most likely because he was able to rest and recover from being injured while the shaggy dog provided for him. I put the shaggy dog back in my car and took him, mom, and pups to a Noah's B'Ark with the hope that they will find the great homes that they deserve and so badly need.

I named the little shaggy dog Hero, a name he truly deserves. He will always have a special place in my heart as I may have only had him in my home for a day, but he has filled the rest of my life with the goodness that's within him. I will cherish all those memories of him running, playing, and protecting all the unloved, unwanted stray dogs and puppies when no one else would.

After this Good Samaritan Ana saved the shaggy little dog, which she named Hero, he was adopted within two weeks by a nice couple but managed to run away from them on the same day. It took Noah's B'Ark rescue volunteers three days to track him down and recapture him. This is where I stepped in.

After hearing his remarkable story, I had to meet this dog. Noah's B'Ark sends many of their adoptees and new pet parents to my training classes to insure they stay in forever homes, so they knew me and allowed me to pull him for observation so I could determine what the best placement for him might be. So on January 2, 2012, I picked Hero up and began working with him as my demonstrational dog and soon realized that this dog needed to have a purpose beyond what the normal pet requires. He was one of those natural-born leaders who would never be happy with just the good life. He needed to help others, and this drive needed to be channeled.

Our educated guess was that Hero is approximately one and a half to two years old and was likely a Poodle mixed with a Schnauzer, a designer dog known as a Snoodle. I decided to train him to be someone's service dog or therapy dog. Training and temperament testing began right away, and I expected it would take me about nine months to fully test and train him for placement if he made it through the challenges of being a full-fledged working dog.

Well, Hero shined brighter than I could have ever imagined in such a short amount of time. He learned to open and close doors, retrieve an array of items, carry things, walk nicely on the leash, sit, stay, come, work off leash, and a whole bunch of other important skills as well as being ready to pass the Assistance Dogs International public access test and the American Kennel Club's Canine Good Citizen's test all by voice command in six months! Now that's a remarkable dog. I can only take credit for bringing it out and giving him the opportunity to shine.

On June 16, 2012, less than seven months after being rescued off the streets of San Jose, California, Hero found his forever home with a wonderful woman named Elizabeth and has become her coworker as she is a psychologist utilizing his amazing compassion and need to help others in her practice with children and adults who are overcoming challenges with the help of a true life Hero. He really has become her coworker in wellness. They also visit care facilities, bringing smiles to people's faces everywhere he goes. He has a beautiful home on ten acres of property and even has three girl dog friends to play with when he is off-duty.

Hero doesn't see himself as remarkable. He just knows he has a purpose in this life, and he intends to fill it with or without our help. We all feel honored to have helped him fulfill his life's purpose. He, like every dog, deserves it. There are countless canine Hero's living in the world. Think of how many go unnoticed and whose lives go on unfulfilled living in backyards or behind closed doors their entire lives. Hoping for the day someone will notice and give them the opportunity to shine just like Hero. Is your dog one of them?

Hero after a bath and a shave. His funny ears makes everyone smile when he looks ready for takeoff! What's not to love?

EPILOGUE

I 'VE NEVER STOPPED seeing nature through the eyes of a child. I am fortunate to have had a mother who made me take notice of the awesome beauty in the natural world that is ever present around us. From the *Undersea World of Jacques Cousteau* to *Mutual of Omaha's Wild Kingdom* and *Marty Stouffer's Wild America*, these televised wildlife specials in the 1970s and 1980s ingrained an appreciation of nature in me that I could have never experienced in a lifetime.

I continue to be influenced even today with National Geographic, Animal Planet, and the Discovery Channel specials. These programs are like virtual reality classrooms in our own living rooms. I can say that I have been around the world over the last forty years exploring the most amazing places and animals on earth all from the comfort of my in home classroom; thanks to those outgoing, risk-taking explorers that found it important enough to take me there with them every week as I could never have gotten this awesome education from anyone but them.

Learning about animals came to me long before learning about myself. It was not Bonnie Bergin or my schooling that first taught me about neuroassociations and the pain and pleasure phenomena. In the mid-1980s, I discovered, through desperation, a popular life coach named Anthony Robbins. I purchased his personal power program from an infomercial and faithfully did what he said since my life was going nowhere but downhill, and I knew *I had to change it* before it continued to change me forever. Anthony Robbins' understanding of how the pain and pleasure neuroassociations phenomenon controls us *is impeccable.* He is still going strong today and is still changing minds using nature's awesome way.

Others like Wayne Dyer, Deepak Chopra, Joyce Meyer, and the late Ernest Holmes all became my "virtual reality" audio-taped mentors and best friends, who rode in my car with me for years, changing my mind (neuroassociations) through their tapes. These people continue to be my inspiration to this day, when I need a good dose of positive reinforcement, since I don't have these influences in my daily life from the "real people" around me, who function at a different pace of existences and have their own problems and stressors to deal with.

What I allow to inspire me today is much different than what I allowed to influence me in my past since my past was marred with negative reinforcement. Seeking out inspiration and positive feedback from others is great when you can find the right inspiration that empowers you. Music is also a natural healer when you chose to listen to messages and tunes that uplifts and encourages your spirit to rise and shine. We seem to be hardwired for it.

I spent all of the 1980s and 1990s undoing the negative associations that were written on my blank slate throughout the 1960s and 1970s. I was fortunate to have met a mentor very early on my journey to wellness named Ralph Miles, who made me realize at age twenty-four that I could never change the past, I can only continue to relive it over and over again by default of what's known as a self-fulfilling prophecy and that I could never change others, I could only change me by thinking for myself. After all, the only constant in your life will always be you. You are stuck living with you the rest of your life, either writing your own story or letting other less-capable people write it for you.

Others will either follow or wallow behind out of fear of change and even try keeping you from advancing and leaving them behind. But you will never move forward unless you start walking your own journey and make your own pathways on foot and in mind because the road is riddled with a lot of wrong turns and dead ends if you allow cruise control to set in and take you there.

But the most important lesson people like Ralph Miles and Anthony Robbins taught me was that *I could rewrite my own slate with the help from balanced mentors* and actually have faith and trust in my own ability to problem-solve and make decisions without having to fear the consequences one faces in the learning process because learning is through experience. I always felt discouraged growing up instead of encouraged when I tried to learn from experience and think for myself.

Failure was emphasized in our family by parents who were ignorant about the psychology of how children learn and thrive. Not much was advertised to the general population back then about the behavioral sciences, so my parents practiced what they felt worked for them. Negative reinforcement was the control mechanism they chose to lead with and assert their dominant leadership over their young. It is how children have been raised for centuries, and my parents were just products of those times.

I believe that I have been able to use my past experience knowing firsthand how negative reinforcement really makes *any being feel* defeated, unmotivated, and frustrated at being unable to be a part of the creative learning process. Just existing day in and day out being led by unstable leaders that make you feel insecure and helpless. I know how a dog feels inside when handled by an unstable handler, and I know how it feels to recondition your mind and overcome this mind-set with good stable mentors that encourage and empower you to succeed. And it's all possible because of the brain's ability to change its physical structure by rewiring itself through neuroplasticity. I have lived it firsthand, and like Anthony Robbins, I know from personal experience it can work for anyone, including your dog, because it's not our way, it's nature's way.

I'm not a writer. I'm just a dog lover that hopes this book sparked some interest in you, wanting to learn more about yourself and man's best friend, because human beings can become a dog's living nightmare when mistreated or misunderstood, and unlike us, they can't turn to another mentor or a life coach to help them succeed. *You are their inspiration and their life coach*, and you took on this responsibility when *you decided* you needed a best friend to share your life with. How you show your appreciation *for this privilege* will determine what you get back from man's best and most loyal friend; as they did not invite you into their life, you invited them to share your life with you. So let go and let dog. You might be surprised at what you learn.

Pawsitively yours,

Margie and Rx Pharmdog Jack

INDEX

responsible guardianship of,
119, 141–51
right choice of, 68–72
and their genetic traits,
21–43, 61–67
and their need for patterns,
51–55
Dyer, Wayne, 186

E

Eddie (dog celebrity), 72–73
Elizabeth (Hero's owner), 183
Epigenetics, 78
eugenics, 25, 32

G

genetic epistemology, 45

H

Hero (dog), 183
Holmes, Ernest, 186

I

Institute of Cytology and
Genetics, 30

K

Knaus, Kerry, 14, 166

L

Lassie (dog celebrity), 72
learning theory, 43

M

Marty Stouffer's Wild America,
185
Mendelian genetics, 29
Meyer, Joyce, 186
Miles, Ralph, 186–87
mind, primitive, 10, 17–20
Moose (dog celebrity). *See*
Eddie (dog celebrity)
*Mutual of Omaha's Wild
Kingdom*, 185

N

neoteny, 62, 79
neuroassociations, 33–35
neurochemistry, 34, 45
neuroplasticity, 47, 129
neuroscience, 48, 50, 75
Noah's B'Ark (pet-rescue
organization), 179, 181–82

O

operant conditioning, 12, 46, 49
Our Amazing World of Nature
(Reader's Digest), 9

P

Parvo (disease), 80
Pavlov, Ivan, 12, 43
pedomorphism. *See* neoteny
Piaget, Jean, 45
Poppins, Mary (fictional
    character), 56
porcupine, 59
potty training (canine), 93–95
Proto Dog, 38
punishment
    negative, 35, 46, 59–60, 151
    positive, 35, 46, 59–60, 151

R

Reader's Digest
    Our Amazing World of
    Nature, 9
reinforcement
    intermittent, 50
    negative, 14, 35, 57–58, 76,
        151, 187
    positive, 14, 35, 57, 59,
        72–73, 76, 97, 151
Robbins, Anthony, 185, 187–88
Rx Pharmdog, 157–61

S

schutzhund (dog sport), 117
Service Dogs for Self-Reliance,
    15, 137
Silver Fox, 28, 30
Skinner, B. F., 12, 49
synapses, 17, 35

T

tabula rasa (theory), 51
tail carriage, 124
tandem repeats, 25

U

Uggy (dog celebrity), 72–73
Undersea World of Jacques
    Cousteau, 185

V

Vulpes vulpes. See silver fox

W

Watson, James, 47–48
Watson, John, 12
Wundt, Wilhelm, 12

Made in the USA
San Bernardino, CA
01 March 2014